All Sides of the Subject

The ATHENE Series

An International Collection of Feminist Books

The Athene Series assumes that all those who are concerned with formulating explanations of the way the world works need to know and appreciate the significance of basic feminist principles.

The growth of feminist research has challenged almost all aspects of social organization in our culture. The Athene Series focuses on the construction of knowledge and the exclusion of women from the process—both as theorists and subjects of study—and offers innovative studies that challenge established theories and research.

On Athene—When Metis, goddess of wisdom who presided over all knowledge was pregnant with Athene, she was swallowed up by Zeus who then gave birth to Athene from his head. The original Athene is thus the parthenogenetic daughter of a strong mother and as the feminist myth goes, at the "third birth" of Athene she stops being Zeus' obedient mouthpiece and returns to her real source: the science and wisdom of womankind.

All Sides of the Subject

Women and Biography

edited by

Teresa Iles

TEACHERS COLLEGE PRESS

Teachers College, Columbia University
New York and London

Published by Teachers College Press, 1234 Amsterdam Avenue,
New York, NY 10027

Library of Congress Cataloging-in-Publication Data

All sides of the subject : women and biography / edited by Teresa
Iles. — 1st ed.
p. cm. — (The Athene series)
Includes bibliographical references and indexes.
ISBN 0-8077-6255-5 (paperback : alk. paper). —
ISBN 0-8077-6256-3 (hardcover : alk. paper)
1. Women's studies—Biographical methods. 2. Biography (as a
literary form) I. Iles, Teresa. II. Series.
HQ1185.A45 1991
809′.93592′082—dc20 90-7895

ISBN 0-8077-6255-5 (paper)
ISBN 0-8077-6256-3 (cloth)

Printed on acid-free paper
Manufactured in the United States of America

99 98 97 96 95 94 93 92 1 2 3 4 5 6 7 8

Contents

Foreword

Dale Spender

Nearly all the contributors to this volume comment on the increasing popularity of women's biography as a genre—and on the absence of research and discussion on its nature and appeal. The contributors speak from personal experience; all are among the new audience for women's biography, all have outlined and explored some facet of the biographical process, and all have realized that they have entered a relatively unchartered area when they have been unable to find guidance as to where they should be going.

There can be no better rationale for a book than that it is greatly needed, and no better motivation for the authors. Each of these contributors has started on her own voyage of discovery and is concerned to point out the notable features, the possibilities and contradictions, in the exciting attempt to explain and explore the fascinating ways of women's biography.

There is no one view of process, product, or response provided here. Women's biography is examined from a variety of perspectives, which helps to extend the range and complexity of the scene. There is an international framework with contributions coming from Britain, the United States, Brazil, Canada, Australia, Japan, Spain, and Norway. There is an interdisciplinary perspective with biographers, fiction writers, sociologists, historians, and literary scholars bringing their own penchants and priorities to the construction of the whole. There is the personal, political perspective which is acknowledged implicitly and explicitly, is an integral part of feminist analysis, and provides much of the light and shade. And of course there is perspective and purpose; while many of the writers are on a common quest to come to terms with the biographical process, they are all forging their own favored paths and making their own assessments for their own individual reasons. This is where Teresa Iles has made such a valuable contribution. In examining the motives for biographical writing, the means by which it may be undertaken, and the measures by which it is judged—by providing an original "glossary" of clarifying and unifying terms—she sets out some of the signposts that make the approach more structured and more satisfying. So while the contributors "go their own way," we are prepared for the overall destination and can appreciate the choices they make on the way.

Some contributors, for example, have focused on a specific subject; they have wanted to learn more about one woman and have found themselves involved in a range of ethical and methodological considerations. At a very basic level, Abi Pirani has come up against the conditions of copyright so that while she has "constructed" her version of Jessie Lipscombe's life, she is constrained from telling much of what she knows publicly. Kathleen Barry has taken on Susan B. Anthony and in profound and provocative style has registered the discrepancy between the received wisdom and the reality of the woman's life; confronted with the contradictory versions she seeks to understand the means by which rebellious women may be rendered innocuous, subdued, and satisfied with their lot in the patriarchal "writing up" that becomes the "truth" for later generations. Rachel Gutiérrez takes this as the starting point for her argument that a characteristic of feminist biography is its analysis of the patriarchal context in which the subject *lived* as well as the patriarchal context in which she was represented, including her life before she attracted attention and was "biographed."

Does the biographer write fact or fiction? Is the subject independent, or a creation of the writer? These are the framing questions for many of the contributions; Pilar Hidalgo compares the "lives" offered by fiction writers with those portrayed by their biographers. There are no simple answers to these questions.

That we need biographies to learn about the collective/individual past of women is a premise that underlies this publication; but *which* women should we study is a specific question addressed by Meryn Stuart. Are only the famous fit for such treatment or is it appropriate to focus on a woman who has been eclipsed? It might be desirable to look for neglected women—who have had claims to fame—and to make an effort to rightfully reinstate them; or in the interest of a more egalitarian and better informed society, it might be preferable to take those who have led ordinary lives, who were unappreciated in their own times, and to give them the status of the heroic.

How to choose one heroine (and how serendipitous is the process) is a question raised by Miriam Kalman Harris, who was determined to reclaim one "lost" woman writer and who, of necessity, became involved in biographical constructions. Judith Jordan takes as her subject a woman who *has* received biographical treatment only to provoke more questions than explanations about her motives.

The nature of the biographer's responsibility to the subject is an issue which cuts across all the contributions but which has special significance when the biographer is a sociological researcher. How life histories can be valuable and how researchers can be ethical are among the problems covered by Anne-Kathrine Broch-Due and Ann Nilsen in their overviews of the role of biography in the construction of social science knowledge.

Liz Stanley starts with *self* as biographer, and reflects on the way that knowledge and the knowledge maker cannot be separated; what are the implications for biographer and biographee if one cannot "exist" without the other? It is Liz Stanley's contention that she is an integral part of the subject she has represented, and that one consequence of this creative process is that the subject is an integral part of the self she has become. Margaret Forster follows in similar vein when she reveals that it was her own experience/reality as a woman which led her to question the accepted accounts of Elizabeth Barrett Browning's life. The problems of having a subject fit the author's view of the world are frankly discussed by Margaret Forster who in fact and in fiction has explored the distinction between the two. Both Liz Stanley and Margaret Forster develop the tantalizing thesis that the biographer's story and the biographee's story share common sources.

Who is reading what, and why, are the concerns of Elizabeth Crawford, one of the few individuals in a position to monitor the popularity of the genre (and its particular trends). How women biographers approach their subjects stylistically is the focus of Liz Dearden. And Takayo Mukai points to the problem of perception (and the power of biography to change lives) in her evocative contribution.

What can be learned from biography is a central consideration of the book. But it is no means a conclusion in terms of the topic. For while *All Sides of the Subject* introduces many new and stimulating biographical issues, so unexplored is the territory that this volume does little more than make known the potential of the research and debate that awaits those who will venture into this area in the future.

It is partly the absence of recorded history that sends women now to women past for the detailed documentation of their daily lives. It is partly because of the way in which biography, "the writing of a life," can synthesize, blend, and transcend the realms of the public and the private that women are fascinated with what the genre can provide. It is partly because women have a literary culture in the developed world, and partly because women have a vested interest in the nature of power and representation—in the construction of silence, in the dynamic distortion and denial—that women want to concentrate on the methodological questions of biography. *All Sides of the Subject* encompasses *and* opens up the significant issues in this remarkable area of study.

Acknowledgments

My first thanks are to Dale Spender for teaching a course on "Writing Women's Biography" in London in July 1988; through it I met and worked with women from a wider world. Thank you also for your ideas and continuing judgment, advice, warmth, and wisdom, mostly from so many miles away; without it all this book would certainly never have happened.

Also I have thanks for the women who participated in that course, many of whom are contributors to this book, and for Liz Stanley whose work on feminist biography has set a trail.

Along the way there have been phone calls, letters, and conversations with women who have, through establishing their own work, set the scene for books such as this and have generously shared their experiences.

In immediate terms I must thank the friends who have encouraged me and shared their feelings and insights with me, particularly Vanessa Bennett, Gail Corbett, Alice Parkin, Ellen Ryan, Sally Ahir, and Lynn Hall. And thanks too to my brother Andrew for his thoughtful assistance and interest throughout.

Chapter 1
Introduction

Teresa Iles

The unexpected discovery in the middle of a woman's life that she could "read" her experience to date in a quite different way, that decisions and choices which had once seemed negative for her could now be showing patterns of profound and satisfying meaning, would be a good enough reason for her to want to know more. A good enough reason to make her curious about many things she had taken for granted as being "just so" in her own and many women's lives.

Sharpened by her own need, she might become aware that when questions were asked about what had "happened" in a particular woman's life, why she had or had not succeeded in her ventures, the answers were biographical, were stories interpreting that life in terms set by the teller. She might wonder what were the possibilities and limitations for writers of women's biography, what were the approaches that had been tried? What were the exciting points for development? What could the knowledge accumulated in recent years within the feminist movement bring to bear on women's biography?

LIFE EXPERIENCE

Discussion of the "experience" of being female in relation to identification as a "woman"—or, conversely, discussion of the differences between women—is implicitly ground in the development of feminist biography. However, biographical work takes place within many disciplines and a biographer could see herself in many ways, including author, editor, biographer, or life history researcher; similarly the person being written about may be addressed in different ways: as informant, subject, character, or biographee. In addition there is the kind of accountability to which the life writer may be held: responsibility to the subject, to a collectivity, to the law, or to herself.

Different traditions define their methods in particular ways, but it may be that some forms are more appropriate to the female subject than others. Abi Pirani describes her biography of Jessie Lipscomb as "my experience of Jessie's life." For her, the writing of the biography was like the experience of getting to know a new acquaintaince, maybe becoming a friend. It was not an accumulation of "facts," unconnected until the moment of writing and reckoning, but was full of the interconnected pains and pleasures of a human encounter. In getting to know a person, the accumulation of more and yet more detailed information, along the lines of a methodical survey-schedule, would make a fool of anyone who was to adopt it as a model for understanding the people she met and interacted with. If the day-to-day responses were not incorporated until the final moment and then offered as a kind of obituary, there would be something unbalanced about the quality of the process.

So, in researching her biography, Margaret Forster describes watching Elizabeth Barrett Browning learn the "womanly" lessons that she also had to learn in her life. Kathleen Barry describes coming to know Susan B. Anthony through learning how she interpreted her experience; in this way "we begin to know our subject the way we know others in our lives."

The closeness and distance between a biographer and her subject is given another perspective by Liz Stanley when she asks "how close are the links between the experience or lives of autobiographers and the written biographies they produce?" This suggests an experiential link between the life of the writer and the way she expresses her understanding of the life of her subject, rather than necessary identification between biographer and biographee. Kathleen Barry emphasizes very definitely that biography is not a case of appropriating the biographee's experience: If she had found her own life within her biography of Susan B. Anthony, "it would have been a false equation." As many writers have emphasized, life experience cannot be located separately from interpretation, and for women writing biography this is also a recognition of the creativity for them of the writing experience.

BIOGRAPHY

How do definitions of the traditional convention of biography engage with the sex of the subject? The Oxford English Dictionary (1989) traces the origins of the word back to its Greek root, "Writing of Lives;" then it categorizes the word under three headings:

> The history of the lives of individual men, as a branch of history.
>
> A written record of the life of an individual.

> The life course of a man or other living being: the life history of an animal or plant. (p. 208)

The reader will draw her own conclusions from the list. As I read it I make connections with the confinement specifically to men's lives in history and literature and to the creation of a written record with emphasis on individual lives in isolation.

The *Current Biography Yearbook* (Charles Moritz, 1988) offers an equally straightforward (superficially at least) account of the kind of emphasis which is admirable in biographical research:

> The aim is to provide the reference librarian, the student or any researcher with brief, objective, accurate and well documented biographical articles about living leaders in all fields of human accomplishment the world over. . . .
>
> Sketches have been made as accurate and objective as possible through careful researching of current biography writers in newspapers, magazines, authoritative reference books, and news releases of both government and private agencies . . . with the exception of occasional interviews, the questionnaires filled out by the biographee remains the primary source of information. (preface)

So unproblematic, so little to discuss, yet at a glance how women would slip through this patriarchal net. Comparing the above description with the introduction (necessarily a good deal longer) to the Dictionary of Women's Biography Jennifer Uglow (1988) begins with an explanation of *why* there should be a dictionary of women's lives (although, from looking at the previous example, the question requires no answer). She then comments on the phenomenon that

> there can be no such thing as an "objective" biographical dictionary of women. First, how can one select from half the human race? Second there is no accepted criteria for excellence implicit in the category itself as there is for artists, politicians or athletes. . . . (p. xvii)

In the face of these intractable problems Jennifer Uglow settles for making explicit the criteria she has developed for selection (which somehow didn't seem necessary in the Yearbook; they were "obvious!"). She also comments on inclusion of Western rather than Eastern women (due to lack or inaccessibility of documentation), which shows at least acknowledgment of an important distortion in what she presents, and also the significance of cultural and personal bias. She makes two other telling (for the purpose of this book) remarks:

> Through the ages biographies have been summoned as evidence in debates about the nature of women; and as the grounds of the debate shift so do the examples. (p. xviii)

> Despite its relatively straight forward educational aim I came to realise that far from presenting a book that was representative of women's experience, I was compiling a book of deviants: independent, odd, often difficult women who had defied the expectations of their society as to what a woman's role should be. (p. xviii)

Carolyn Heilbrun (1989) puts it in this way:

> When biographers come to write the life of a woman—and this phenomenon has, of course, occurred with much greater frequency since the advent of contemporary feminism, let us say since the the late 1960's—they have had to struggle with the inevitable conflict between the destiny of being unambiguously a woman and the woman subject's palpable desire, or fate, to be something else. Except when writing about queens, biographers of women have not therefore been at ease with their subjects—and even with queens, like Elizabeth I of England, there has been a tendency to see them as somewhat abnormal, monstrous. It is no wonder that biographers have largely ignored women as subjects, and that critics of biography have written as though men were the only possible subjects. (p. 21)

WRITERS, READERS, AND SUBJECTS (WAYS OF SEEING AND THE CONSEQUENCES)

Discussion about the processes and purposes of feminist biography makes evident the different starting points, the different language, that can divide women working within academic and popular conventions. Consequences of working from particular premises arise for the writer, the reader, and the subject.

If She Sees Herself as Biographer

According to convention the biographer sees herself as using the results of research into a woman's life to write her story. Victoria Glendinning (1988) has termed it "fiction under oath." She is under oath to be true to the evidence, but equally to be true to herself in her interpretation, for there will always be resonances between herself and her subject: moments of recognition, rejection, and surprise. In her biography, Margaret Forster (1988) uses this awareness to create the first meeting of Elizabeth Barrett Browning with Robert. Sifting through what she knows of them, having read their letters and so on, she draws on her own feelings about how they might have been with each other on that first day. Projection certainly, but employed with a clear and honest purpose, and openly accountable to the reader.

A biographer knows she is constructing a story from whatever evidence she has: sometimes there is so much that she could wish there were less, sometimes there is so little that the imaginative task is substantial. Fay Weldon's (1985) *Rebecca West* is catalogued as fiction; it concerns the time (that had not often been written about) around the birth of Rebecca's son, Anthony—a time when Rebecca was isolated from friends, family, and lover and could perhaps have found comfort in a sympathetic voice from the future. The book consists of Weldon's "letters" to Rebecca:

> I have the temerity to write to you—and temerity it is—only because you are so young. I would certainly not write to you in your later years about such subjects as love, life and married men. What could I know compared to you? (p. 27)

So the reader is presented with a "fictional" dialogue through which a "real" story can nevertheless be told. Fay Weldon's "fictional" biography has a "real" setting in Rebecca West's life, but it is her own letters that the reader directly engages with, rather than the "historical" documents of Rebecca herself, it is fiction rather than research. Or is it simply another side of the same process?

If She Sees Herself as Author

When the author is happy to emphasize her own responsibility for creating the "characters" in her story, she is avowedly a writer of fiction. The line to be trodden here is fine and very fascinating. The author creates characters, dramatic characters, whose lives are bounded entirely within the story; accountability for what is presented would be in terms of perspective and possibility rather than a literal concept of factuality. So, within fiction, Toni Morrison's (1987) acclaimed novel *Beloved* recreates a historical time (around the abolition of slavery in the United States) through telling the interconnected stories of people who "live" now in history for her readers. In "fact," documents of their lives would rarely have been preserved, other than as "cases," or "types."

Paradoxically, it is certain that readers can find themselves in works of fiction, sometimes literally, when a writer works on contemporary themes and the "characters" are transparently "real" to those who know her well; sometimes though it is through a more diffuse recognition. Certainly some "fictions" will have had powerful effects on real relationships, and conversely it has been observed not infrequently that novels may be fictionalized biographies. Brenda Maddox (1989) puts this into her own perspective when she writes in her biography of Nora Joyce: "there is much to be learned about Nora's thoughts from Joyce's work but it can only be speculative. The bar between biography and fiction must remain" (p. 499). Fay Weldon, as already mentioned, would argue the point, and Victoria Glendinning would find a further way of working with the paradox. This is certainly a place where the definitions are not mutually exclusive:

> In recent years biography as a genre has come under a good deal of close scrutiny. Roland Barthes has called biography "a novel that dare not speak its name," and the understanding that biographies are fictions, constructions by the biographer of the story she or he had to tell, has become clear. In all disciplines, particularly history, scholars have lately written about how much of what passes for history is in fact evidence from the prevailing or established opinion of the age under consideration or, as likely, of the age in which the author of the history lives. (Heilbrun, 1989, p. 30)

If She Sees Herself as Researcher

A researcher writes under pressures of a different kind—the most acute being perhaps her commitment to a reader, whose interest is academic, and whose priorities in judging her work will be bound up with criteria for scholarly presentation. It is easy to see how an overarching scholarly brief could be an inappropriate form for a biography, tending toward the monumental and militating against the presentation of a life in human dimensions: no greater, no smaller. On the same theme, it has been pointed out by more than one modern biographer that the conventional format of text followed by extensive notes spread over many pages (the latter appended to make the reader believe the former) could have quite the opposite effect from that intended, suggesting a show of uncertainty rather than of confidence. By implication also, the positioning of such notes draws attention away from the process of interpretation which gives shape to the biography.

Both in sociological research and in biographical research quotations carry privilege as a method of "getting at" experience and subjectivity. Ironically though, as social researcher Ann Game (1989) comments:

> Through the use of quotation "the subjective becomes the objective, experience the referent, and the speech of the interview the transparent medium of experience . . . what frequently went unacknowledged was the position of the researcher, the fantasies and projections involved, the ways in which interviews are produced by the interviewer. (p. 344)

Fay Weldon, as already mentioned, reverses this process, showing how thoroughly the writer is the subject of the interpretations she produces. However, within feminist research models there can be found influences at work which make necessary recognition of the subjective, or rather the intersubjective, in human studies: Kathleen Barry links her biographical research with "saturation" in the kind of life history research described by Ann Nilsen and Anne Kathrine Broch-Due.

If She Sees Herself as Editor

An editor acknowledges the process of selection and valuation with which she is involved in constructing a text and creating a biography. There are so many facets excluded, which another editor might have picked on as "the main story" of the day. She relies on her sense of what is relevant and awaits a response with interest.

As biographer, author, or researcher, she is also an editor, and has the power to choose her version. She can use quotations in different ways, she can present her subject in stereotypical manner, she can make her into a victim, she can make her misconstrued, she can decide who to talk to, and to whom to give credence in the way she sets out her story. The biographer always edits, and this can be presented as an open part of the writing (hence "leaving a trail," as Meryn Stuart describes, following the work of Liz Stanley). Awareness of the impact of what is left out is considered by Carolyn Heilbrun (1989) as she quotes Phyllis Rose:

> But there is no neutrality. There is only greater or less awareness of one's bias. And if you do not appreciate the force of what you're leaving out, you're not fully in command of what you're doing. (p. 30)

WHAT THE BIOGRAPHEE CAN EXPECT

If Her Writer Sees Her as Subject

The biographee could reasonably expect to be able to look back at the writer from within the text; that is, it will always be clear that she is separate from the representation of her, and cannot be "made sense of" as though she were a riddle to be guessed, solved, and put aside for the next. She can expect to see her writer respond to knowing her, maybe to watch her learn, certainly to recognize herself as being moved in a variety of ways. She may be "named," in which case she can call upon the law to protect her.

If Her Writer Sees Her as Informant

The biographee can expect to be taken account of as one source of information in a research process, but in no way can she expect what she says to influence the format of the inquiry; she will be seen as having the answers to particular problems that her writer has defined, she may even herself be considered to be a "problem" by her writer. She gives her information and is left while it is processed through a bureaucratic system. Does she recognize herself if she sees the outcome; has she become a "type," a composite character and if so is it fact or fiction? She could give her opinion on it if she were asked. How will it be used? What is it for? She may never know! She may wonder why she was chosen: Was it because she was ordinary (and is that all right) or is she strange, unusual, a freak in some way she had not noticed before. She could expect to remain anonymous, though the researcher could become well known.

If She Recognizes Herself as "Character"

The biographee in someone's novel will probably remain anonymous, although if her author is well known the sources may be researched and written about. She may be seen as having "biographical interest" through her association with another person's life; if that person is a woman, many more choices are opening in the depiction.

CROSSING THE DISCIPLINES

Writing women's biography is full of double binds, as Jennifer Uglow (1982) suggested in the Dictionary of Women's Biography. The contributors to this book are working from the premise that women's lives should be written—and all kinds of women, not just the exceptions to "prove the rule." Interestingly, in questioning the absence of women from representation in so many different traditions, they find that they can create a space for their subjects through acknowledging the falseness of those separations, a falseness that become obvious when women's lives are put in the center of the research. When the overlapping ground between the categories of fiction, social history, psychological observation, and sociological insight is recognized as fertile rather than dangerous, for a biographer, because it contains contradictions in the very roots of knowledge, it can work very well for women whose lives also contradict the validity of this knowledge.

For instance Flora Thompson's (1939/1985) *Larkrise to Candleford* is a work of fiction that could be read as biography (about a child, Laura, growing up in England at the turn of the last century) and as autobiography (transparently about the life of the author herself). This might seem to be introducing unnecessary complications, but acknowledging that the separate analytic traditions accrued by different kinds of knowledge do not have either to exclude or to subordinate each other in order to coexist; taken together in practice they may indeed support each other to create quite special kinds of insight.

In her writing, Flora Thompson's method is historical: She charts the social changes that are taking place during Laura's childhood. It is fictional: She accepts that she is using her imagination in making Laura's story into a narrative that she creates in league with her memory and in tow to her need for expression. She has achieved a rare goal of being widely read, although her subject could seem unremarkable except to her own self.

It is no accident that Flora Thompson wrote in the form that she did, it was a form in which she could recognize herself and feel comfortable; she could not embark on the same study and call it history, although undoubtedly it must now be considered a rich contribution within that tradition. As a woman writer what she has achieved is special because she allows not only her characters to be known as she tells her story, she also reveals herself as a female thinker. She has left the means of knowing her in writing; she can be known in her mind and in her emotionality, known in her critical awareness and through her astute reflections on the times in which she lived. By skillfully using the role of the narrator or storyteller, she establishes herself as the self-conscious "observer" of the social circumstances in which she was formed and lived. She crosses the divide between disciplines and delivers to her characters the respect they deserve as her correspondents.

How is the space created, and what kind of knowledge is it? In *Larkrise to Candleford* the reader is addressed by the sensory intensity of Laura's responses and is drawn into reflection on them not by means of sociological abstraction, nor by forcing them into some kind of psychological developmental schedule, but by looking back after the passage of time, the passage of life, and drawing the meanings from the author's life as she constructs it. The separate space that a view from a different time and place give her is not the same thing as a claim to objectivity, nor to a definitive, authoritative version. A dialogue between Flora, the adult woman in the later years of her life, and Laura, the child who once was herself, creates a distance that allows a story to be told; the story of her own development as she chooses to tell it and in relation to the people she lived with and the social circumstances they shared.

Laura's wondering curiosity can make no claim to a full understanding of the world, but she interrogates it with her own way of seeing; often what she records is straightforward puzzlement about the gap between her own perception and the seeming authoritative explanations given her by adults. It is after a passage of time that her own reflections lead to the development in her of a powerful self-knowledge. Flora's valuation of the conversations of inner life give structure to her narrative, make it philosophical and psychological, as well as historical, literary, and popular: a rare achievement for a woman of rural origins who valued her own thoughts and wished to express them in the medium that she had grown to love.

Using a device that women have often used, Flora reflects on her own life as though she were an outsider, and tells it in that way: as the biography (or story) of someone else. It is the inverse of a biographical approach that—through research and imagination—explores another person's life as though from the inside. The two practices are clearly not the same, but they are related ways of taking on the richly complex process of telling life stories.

There is a contrast between writing that is self-consciously expressive and writing that sterilizes connections. So much of knowledge can be presented in connected and creative ways; it is these matters of choice and valuation that particularly interest and challenge feminist biographers of women in the following pages.

REFERENCES

Forster, Margaret. (1988). *Elizabeth Barrett Browning*. London: Chatto & Windus.

Game, Ann. (1989). *Journal of Pragmatics 13* (pp. 343–361). Elsevier Science Publishers B.V.. (North-Holland).

Glendinning, Victoria. (1988, July 21). Public lecture. University of London, Women's Studies Summer Institute.

Heilbrun, Carolyn. (1989). *Writing a woman's life*. London: Women's Press.

Maddox, Brenda. (1989). *Nora: A biography of Nora Joyce*. London: Mandarin.

Morrison, Toni. (1987). *Beloved*. London: Chatto & Windus.

Moritz, Charles (Ed.). (1988). *Current biography yearbook*. New York: H. W. Wilson.

Oxford English Dictionary. (1989). Oxford: Clarendon Press.

Thompson, Flora. (1939/1985). *Larkrise to Candleford*. Harmondsworth: Penguin.

Uglow, Jennifer. (1982). *Dictionary of women's biography*. London: Macmillan.

Weldon, Fay. (1985). *Rebecca West*. Harmondsworth: Penguin.

Part 1
Issues

As the excitement of finding a subject settles, what are the problems that arise? There are plenty of practical problems, for example: Who "owns" the material that you want to use—the letters, photographs, diaries; can you look at them? Can you publish them? It's better to sort out copyright before embarking on a project that might later prove to be futile—if you are not allowed to make public what you have found out!

And there are the challenges that come set in the material itself: If there are many "versions" of the subject's life, whose do you "believe?" Are they all valid? Who has the facts and who the fictions? As some of these contributions show, it can be profitable to think about the questions, even to do some research in this area before undertaking the project. It is easier to evaluate the "evidence" when you have a framework for evaluation.

The writers in this section each explore the above themes in the context of their own work on biography. Abi Pirani and Kathleen Barry write about how they did their research and their ways of conceptualizing what was happening as they got to know their subjects. Pilar Hidalgo and Rachel Gutiérrez write on untangling the "facts" of the lives of particular women, in relation to their achievements in the literary and artistic worlds, and the relevance of biography to this task.

Chapter 2

Sources and Silences

Abi Pirani

At the present time, the archive of materials relating to Jessie Lipscomb (1861–1952) are protected by copyright laws. While respecting the family's right to protect the material, my own relationship with Jessie is mine to recount, experience, and share. For a biography and further explanation, please see the notes and references.

LOOKING FOR JESSIE

Jessie? Yes, I know Jessie. Well, she's sort of . . . a friend . . . a companion. . . .

We share so many things. We are both women, both artists, and both mothers. We are also both white, privileged, educated, and creative people. We are very different too. For one thing, she is dead—died three years before I was born. And she was born in another century, another world, another lifetime. Many of the differences in our lives are balanced by the similarities; Jessie set up a resonance for me that even now surprises me.

There is a lot I can tell you about her. There is a lot more I cannot. I can give you a skeleton, buried under blue Welsh slate in a tiny churchyard, facts of parentage, student life, marriage, four children. Then there is the rest of her, gone now, that I can flesh out with imagination, common ground, shared interests, impressions, her son's and her grandson's memories.

What I cannot do is break copyright. So if you stand before a mirror with me, we may both catch a glimpse of Jessie, a partial reflection, protected by law, hidden in time. That reflection is one that Jessie and I share. As I look in the mirror I see her eyes looking back at me, she is a part of myself now. I created the affinity with an introductory sketching, many sketches, never a finished portrait, more an autobiographical study—my experience of Jessie's life.

Looking for Jessie, I walked through Paris and Peterborough, wrote to public offices all over the country, searched for documents in archives and libraries, studied the sculpture and lives of Camille Claudel and Auguste Rodin.

Most recently (May 1989), I watched the French film of Camille Claudel which was overwhelming and illuminating, a different perspective from my own. Camille's silence has been broken, Camille is now public property in France; books, speculation, articles, exhibitions, and the three-hour film. There is not room here to talk too long about Camille, but she did introduce me to Jessie, so her story has some bearing on mine.

Camille was an extraordinarily talented sculptress who, like Gwen John some years later, got too involved with the well-known artist Auguste Rodin. Camille's family had her institutionalized and she died after thirty years in a mental asylum. Nineteenth-century France had little time for a woman who had an abortion, a child, or both, by a man she was not married to, particularly if that woman was also an artist. So it was for Camille.

My experience would make a different film; one that stressed women's friendship, that saw Camille as Jessie saw her, a friend in youth and old age, a part of the life that Jessie loved. What the film explores well is woman as artist, working with clay, with onyx and marble, finding the "people who were inside the stone."

The film also touches on Jessie and Camille's friendship in Paris in the 1880s. I looked beyond that time: to Camille, incarcerated in a mental asylum for thirty years, lonely and unhappy; and to Jessie, married with the responsibilities of four children and a large house and garden. Neither woman produced much work in later life. Both, for very different reasons, were restricted in art practice, limited by society and family: a sorrow they shared.

Exploring the pathways, walking the streets of Jessie's life, sensing the air she breathed, I draw something of her into myself, and slowly, painfully, birth it, nurture it, allow it—her—Jessie—to be alive, strong, powerful, and trustworthy.

Why trustworthy? Mainly because Jessie is, in a very real sense, my own creation. And I know I can trust that. I hear a truth, a voice, explore and share it, give flesh and color to wasted skeletons, memories. I am persuaded of the validity of her reality, of mine. We have shared something of the same lilting music . . . and the same deafening silences.

Silence

Speaking out about women's lives, we break silence. Silence is that powerful and restrictive protection, particularly enforced by our patriarchal society, that hides so many truths, so many "herstories."

My story of Jessie is now 5 years old. The beginning was unexpected, two photographs in the catalog from the 1984 Paris exhibition of Camille Claudel (Camille Claudel, 1984). The first picture shows Jessie with Camille; both student artists in Paris, young women in worksmocks, smoking and drinking tea in the *atelier*. I felt an atmosphere of hard work and enjoyment, my own feelings about being at college, having the luxury and time to do what one loves, enjoying a chat between work sessions.

The second picture was from nearly 50 years later. Jessie is elderly, visiting Camille, an unhappy woman whose own incredible story was included in the catalog, and is explored in depth in the film. In this photograph, Jessie is well-dressed and gently serene; life has not treated her badly, she gazes contentedly into the camera. Camille looks weary, wrapping unused hands around herself, her head tilted to one side, a moving portrait by Jessie's husband, William.

I was intrigued and curious. I had a feeling of certainty, as yet unfounded, that there was more than I could see, that Jessie had her own story to tell, one that was interesting and valuable. The lifetime between the two pictures ensnared me. What had happened for Jessie in that time? Why had I never heard of her name? Even a minor artist has a life, a network of events and decisions that makes her unusual, particularly in the restrictive environment of 19th-century Britain. The question marks flooded me.

And why this connection with the brilliant, tempestuous, beautiful, and unstable Camille, a sculptor with unusual talent, a woman of strange and complex experience? What persuaded Jessie to look for Camille in later life, to visit her, to acknowledge her concern about Camille's circumstances within the asylum? What were the strengths of this 50-year friendship?

These original question marks are, in many ways, still there. It has taken 5 years to build up the story of Jessie's life, and much of the information about Camille is now more available than it was 5 years ago. Given the quality and breadth of the Jessie Lipscomb Archive, it would be possible to explore the two women's friendship through a film, TV documentary, or a book.

Jessie's perspective, particularly of Camille, would provide a fascinating view of women artists' lives and friendships. The material about Jessie covers the last 150 years and includes her history and experience, letters, photographs, and documents. She is seen as an artist in Paris and provincial England; there are fragments of Jessie and Camille's friendship.

Looking back from now, 1989, to myself in 1984 staring and frowning at Jessie's face, I am still surprised at my tenacity and determination to find Jessie. Many things are still unclear, but I hang onto our relationship, as if I have promised her to clear the mystery up like any good detective—for that is what I became. Researching Jessie's life, I began at the beginning. I had never tackled research before, and found out many things in the long way round. Over the months the clues mounted up: facts, coincidences, and lucky breaks.

TIME IN PARIS

One of the strangest things of all in the research has been jumping backwards and forwards through the 19th and 20th centuries. The time trap is a complex thing. I read a lot of science fiction, and am very conscious of the instability of time. Time takes on a new meaning in a research project of this type. Looking for the "facts" of an individual's life, hunting down her relatives—usually male—and piecing together the bits of information to try and create a recognizable pattern distorts time as we are led to expect it.

Like so many women, Jessie became known as "wife of . . . and mother of . . ." This distortion is common. It took me an awful long time to find Jessie through either her maiden or married name, and then the task was made easier by her son being in *Who's Who,* and his middle name being her maiden name.

Sometimes I would have to wait months, even a year, to follow up a lead, or get a letter that put another piece into place. Sometimes I would look anxiously at Jessie and tell her it was impossible, I was stuck, and why on earth did it matter anyway? And every now and then there would be that imaginary boom of drums or thunder as things dropped neatly into place, delivering insights and awareness, generating new leads.

I developed a considerable respect for the people who work in the public offices of Britain: people who, given the right information, would dredge up impossibly obscure documents relating to birth, baptism, marriage, and death. The Public Offices network is not subtle and yet somehow it is hidden from us. It is a network full of opposites: of disappointment and joy, of public and private. Across the country it is housed in buildings of formal application, curtained with hushed corridors and crowded shelves. Externally these rooms proclaim "Registrar" and "Records", "Archives" and "Library". The premises are often ornately Victorian, an image shattered by modern offices and upheld by ancient letterheads . . . (York, 1987). I became adept at the kind of letterwriting and interpretation necessary to deal with the information. Jessie was changing me, from her grave, allowing me to develop skills I was previously unaware of, persuading me into situations I would otherwise not have dealt with.

The most important of these situations, perhaps for both me in 1985, and Jessie in 1884 to 1885, was going to Paris. The day I left, I had one of those strange "coincidental" happenings that made me smile ruefully to myself, recognizing the uncanny certainty I had of following a trail already signposted for me.

I stood on the local station platform, waiting for the first train of my journey to Paris. I was uncertain about going abroad for 2 weeks on my own, living alone in Paris, staying in a foreign country, looking for a woman in another century.

There was a whistle down the line, and a roar of churning wheels and billowing smoke. A steam train roared through the Victorian station, gleaming, proud, wheels spinning, carriages rocking. Past and present were fused momentarily. Was it 1985, or 1885? I felt Jessie stood on a similar platform with her bags, travelling to her future, which was my past. The smoke hung in the tunnel, I watched it, bemused.

I experienced Paris as an art student and a sculptor, much as Jessie would have done. I looked at art nearly every day—in the streets, in the shops, in the galleries. Jessie was in Paris for 4 consecutive years, staying each time with Camille. I followed Jessie and Camille's trail—the places they had lived and worked, the streets they had walked. Camille's last home in Paris was on the edge of the Seine. Today the street corner is marked only by a single tree and a Victorian streetlamp. I felt Camille's isolation in a big city, and Jessie's excitement as the life of Paris took hold. Then and now, Paris is a city for artists.

In 1987, I researched the experiences of women artists in Paris at the turn of the century. Many women were drawn to the city from across Europe, studying a wide range of subjects in a liberally minded and exciting city. Among the artists of Jessie's generation there were some familiar names. Most were painters—student painters who wrote articles of their daily lives, their models, and their masters. They worked hard, living simply, "a Bohemian life:" Jessie's environment over 4 years.

I followed Mary Cassatt into the drawing room with her mother and her sister. Gwen John and Paula Modersohn-Becker were in their studios, working with quiet intensity. Suzanne Valadon was there, both the artist and the model. Through the diaries of Marie Bashkirtseff (1890), I saw Paris itself and its daily life for an artist. I watched Kathe Kollwitz study sculpture and go to the museums, enjoying the sights, the people, and the city.

While in Paris myself, I experienced the environment of Paris as it is now, the art galleries and market stalls, stained-glass in churches and fine sculpture in parks, wide boulevards and narrow alleys, many artists and pedlars working outside on the streets. Of 19th-century Paris, I include the following extracts written by Marie Bashkirtseff (1890) and Kathe Kollwitz (1955), there are many other sources (Marie Adelaide Belloc, 1887; E. O. Somerville, 1886).

Paris, 1877

Thursday, October 4th. The day passes quickly when you are drawing from eight till twelve, and from one till five. Going backwards and forwards takes up nearly an hour and a half, and then I was a little late, so that I only had six hours' work. . . . All I have done till now has been but a sorry jest! . . .

[M. Julian] says that sometimes his female students are as clever as the young men. I should have worked with the latter, but they smoke—and besides, there is no advantage. There was when women had only the draped model; but since they make studies from the nude, it is just the same.

Saturday, October 6th. I have seen no one, as I have been at the studio.

I am getting rather used to their ways—their artistic ways.

In the studio all distinctions disappear; you have neither name nor family; you are no longer the daughter of your mother; you are yourself; you are an individual with art before you—art and nothing else. One feels so happy, so free, so proud!

Wednesday, November 14th. I have been to the neighbourhood of the Ecole de Medicine, to get various books and plaster casts. I went to Vasser's. You know Vasser, who sells all kinds of anatomical models, skeletons, &c. . . .

I am enchanted: the streets are full of students coming out from the schools. These narrow streets! these musical instrument makers, and all that kind of thing! Ah, heavens! how well I understood the magic, if I may call it so, of the Quartier Latin! . . . Speak to me of the Quartier Latin, and welcome. It is there that I feel reconciled to Paris. (Marie Bashkirtseff, 1890, pp. 274–290)

Paris, 1904

Paris enchanted me. In the mornings I went to the old Julien school for the sculpture class, in order to familiarize myself with the fundamentals of sculpture. Afternoons and evenings I visited the wonderful museums of the city, the cellars around the markets or the dance halls on Montmartre or the Bal Bullier.

We used to take our evening meal in one of those big cafes on Boulevard Montparnasse where the artists ate en masse, sitting together by nationalities.

Paris held me fast until the very last evening. (Kathe Kollwitz, 1955, pp. 44–45)

It was the flavor of Paris that changed the lives of many women, including Jessie. Later in her life she was somehow isolated, separated from her neighbors by experience and an insight into an unusually vibrant world of color and light.

When I spoke to Jessie's eldest son, a few months before his death at age 96, he remembered his mother's love of Paris, and being sculpted by her as a boy. Speaking to Jessie's son was, in itself, a distortion of time. I was so close to his mother, even though I had never met her; he was born to her in another century, a distant world away.

A year later, I was invited by Jessie's grandson to explore the Archive materials held by him. Once again, past and present were to meet.

Jessie's grandson gave full access to the Archive for the purposes of my Master of Art but now wishes to use the material himself, as part of his family's history. His contribution would offer an interesting and personal appreciation of Jessie's life.

I would still like the opportunity to make public my findings, and concentrate on Jessie's life as an artist and friend of Camille. As a woman and an artist, I feel that my story of Jessie would appeal to a different audience and see Jessie from an equally valuable and interesting perspective.

STILL ARCHIVES

I had no idea what, or how much I would find. I had 2 months before my MA Dissertation was to be handed in, and many bits of information needing links. Each time the research reached a new turning point everything had to be reassessed and redefined, depending on the nature of the new information.

It was to prove to be a researcher's dream, the kind of experience one has but once: two trunks piled chaotically with dusty documents, letters, and momentos; sculptures of Jessie's from the 1880s to the 1920s; and the space and time to search and photograph, photocopy, and record all that I could. Jessie's grandson was very interested in what I turned up, offering names to photographs and background to letters.

The most valuable aspect of the Archive was that, at some time in the past, someone had put in many things about Jessie's life, as if they had known it might be of interest. I worked intensely for 2 days and most of 2 nights as well!

The results are in my dissertation and in files, the tiniest details of Jessie's life, the complications of daily existence, the landmarks, the joys, and the sorrows. Because William, Jessie's husband, was a good, amateur photographer, there is an unexpected wealth of visual materials, photographs over the years, such as the two in the Claudel catalog (Claudel, 1984). Unlike the families of many women, Jessie's relatives have had the space to store her history, work, and the story of her life up to the days before her death: all sorts of memorabilia treasured and protected.

Archives are like stills from a film—individual pictures which, run together, tell a rich and fascinating story. This Archive encompassed Jessie's life, from around 1880 to January, 1952 when she died. A diary used by Jessie's daughter-in-law gave a moving account of the last 12 days before her death. When Jessie died, her husband William, aged 91, collapsed, and died 8 days later. Not surprisingly, the diary was little used afterwards.

Accepting Jessie's death was hard. I had spent so long trying to create an image of her, and yet I could never meet her. I found myself mentally mourning her loss, feeling a sense of grief.

Looking at the blue, Welsh slate gravestone in a tiny churchyard, I watched the light play through the trees. It was peaceful. Something with life could come out of Jessie's death, something Jessie and I shared. Across the strange boundaries of time, we are both women, artists, and mothers. We share a love of our children and of clay. As women we share experiences that all women share.

I had seen so much of Jessie's life, got as close as I could to her reality. Even though she herself was not there, I had enough to describe her. During those 3½ years of research I had been all around the house Jessie had lived in—built by her father—seen something of the Paris she had known, walked the streets of her home town, sat at her graveside, and talked with her son and her grandson.

Of Jessie as a sculptor I have deliberately said little. I am not trained to assess the quality of her sculptures, or their place in history, but I like her work. I understand her need to sculpt, and continue to wonder if there is any more of her work anywhere. The Archive holds some 20 pieces, including, most interestingly, a head of Jessie by Camille, and one of Camille by Jessie (Claudel, 1984).

Once again, I speculated about their relationship, I liked the idea of the two women working together on mutual portraits. I felt that they had enjoyed their friendship, and that that alone would be sufficient reason for Jessie to look for Camille in later years.

MISSING PERSONS

I pulled most of the experiences together and presented them for the MA with the title *Jessie: Study of an Artist*. At this point copyright was withheld, which prevented my taking things any further. With hindsight I know that I put everything away safely, waiting for something to happen. All through, time had proved unstable, why should it now prove otherwise?

Nothing happened for a year. I followed other interests, involved myself in my own creative work, looked after my children, continued to struggle with similar problems to those experienced by Jessie and many others. The pull between the creative art work and the creative home-based work continued. In that way women's experience has changed little. I faced this every day, constantly reminded of the past, working to change the future.

I looked too, to women's networks, and for women's friendship, recognized the potential and quality of them. My experience of Jessie's life had led me to make unexpected decisions about my own life, had changed and enriched me, had encouraged me to explore more fully the value of other women's experience and the effects on my own.

Jessie resurfaces when the time is right, as it is now. When asked to write about the "process" of biography, I found myself struggling to express the creativity involved. This chapter has been an attempt to put in a straight line, something of the spider's web involved in gathering, interpreting, and communicating my perspective of Jessie Lipscomb's life.

The creative process of biography allows a close interaction between the participants, even if some of them are dead. The facts state that Jessie, and many of the others in her life, died years ago. Recreating her, and the others, has been fascinating, disturbing, slow, and enthralling. It has been a real life process for me, I can see Jessie in my mind's eye, I recognize her. The imagined reality:

> Jessie put down her pen. The wet ink glowed on the page as she reached across her writing desk. She looked out of the study window as she took an envelope and stuck a stamp on it. The garden looked beautiful from here in the evening. Behind her, William's chair was close to the fire. Books lined the small room, softening the voices of father and son. Jack was waiting to take the letter to the post, he and William talked quietly.
>
> Syd would get the letter tomorrow if it went now.
>
> The evenings were getting colder, Jessie made a mental note to order coal and candles, corn for the hens; the needs of the household took her attention once again. She rubbed her hands together quickly and turned from the desk. "Here you are Jack. Go carefully now, there could be a frost tonight."
>
> The room went quiet. Jessie picked up another sheet of notepaper. She would write to Helen, in London. The small glass panes in her writing desk reflected the firelight. (Abi Pirani, 1987)

Watching the film of Camille Claudel I was riveted. Jessie was now even closer, she had a film personality—not quite as I see her—but she was there. So too was Camille, played brilliantly by Isabelle Adjani. The film concentrated, in my view, on the creative struggle, the battle of being the artist and the woman. Camille the artist fought hard and produced marvelous sculptures, but Camille the woman faced all the prejudices of her day, and, unsupported, had no strength left.

The film finishes with William's marvelous portrait of Camille, taken in the asylum when he and Jessie visited her there. The photograph itself is a moving tribute to Camille, as is the film. I was conscious of all the later years in the asylum missing from the film, Jessie's hunt for Camille and William's other sensitive photograph of the two women together. Hospital records are 9ot available yet in full, however, the rest of the story must one day be told.

I feel that Jessie's life story and world view are worth following through. In a sense this chapter is incomplete, as I do not feel that there has been a conclusion to Jessie's story. We have, as it were, unfinished business; if Jessie is a ghost, she haunts me still.

The first time I wrote about Jessie I called the article "The Joy of Recognition" (Abi Pirani, 1985); it is that feeling that I keep with me, that supports me through the footwork and the waiting; for that I delve into archives and sources, and break into the silence.

POSTSCRIPT

Kathe Kollwitz once said that as an artist she had the right to extract the emotional content from a situation, and should not have to be involved with the politics of it. I feel much the same about the issue of copyright material.

I respect the right of the family to use the material as they want, however, I feel that the issue of copyright is one of freedom of information, not profit. Of course I would like to earn money from my research—I am still in the lowpaid, self-employed bracket!

It is the silencing of women's voices, either deliberately or inadvertently, that results from the restrictions of copyright which concerns me more. Information about women's lives, particularly but not exclusively in the past, is often difficult to find.

As artists, women are particularly susceptible to misappropriation and disappearance. Their work has been claimed to be that of a male artist of their time, or the women are labelled as having the talent of a man. Many women artists have given up after marriage and did not exhibited their early work.

Today, women artists and their work are receiving a growing recognition, but there is still a long way to go:

> The works of women need exposure; they need sharing with their largest possible audience to develop a special vocabulary of appreciation and the same joy of recognition that men's art has received over the centuries. (Karen Petersen & J. J. Wilson, 1978, p. 10)

Finding Jessie was an intensely personal search, where being a woman was very important. As Jessie's family has had enough space to keep all the materials, her Archive is particularly rich in local and personal history and fascinating visual materials.

I simply regret being unable to share what I have seen with the largest possible audience. One woman's story can be a powerful insight into our own lives.

REFERENCES

Bashkirtseff, Marie. (1985). *The journals of Marie Bashkirtseff.* (M. Blind, Trans.) London: Virago. (Original work published 1890)

Belloc, Marie Adelaide. (1887). Lady artists in Paris. *Murray's Magazine, 8*(45), 371–384.

Claudel, Camille. (1984). Exhibition catalogue, Musee Rodin. Paris.

John, Gwen. (1985). An interior life. Exhibition catalogue. The Barbican Centre, London.

Kollwitz, Kathe. (1955). *The diary and letters.* Ed. Hans Kollwitz. Trans. R and C Winston Chicago: H. Regnery.

Petersen, Karen, Wilson, J. J. (1978). *Women artists: A recognition and reappraisal from the Middle Ages to the 20th century.* London: Women's Press.

Pirani, Abi. (1985). Introductory paper. Unpublished thesis, Bradford College, Bradford, England.

Pirani, Abi. (1987). Jessie: study of an artist. Unpublished Dissertation, York University.

Somerville, E. O. (1886). An atelier des dames. *The Magazine of Art, 9,* 152–157.

Chapter 3

Toward a Theory of Women's Biography: From the Life of Susan B. Anthony

Kathleen Barry

In 1897, while Elizabeth Cady Stanton was preparing her memoirs, she wrote to Susan B. Anthony:

> Dear Susan,
>
> I do think in this earlier part of your life there should be some mysterious or undefined references to some faint suffering love affair. If your sisters can glean any facts in that line from your true inwardness, nothing could be more agreeable to me than to weave a sentimental chapter entitled, for instance, "The Romance of Susan B. Anthony's Younger Days." How all the daily papers would jump at that! (Theodore Stanton & Harriot Stanton Blatch, 1922)

Stanton had a reason for wanting to create a new image of her best friend. During their time, Anthony and women like her—women who refused to be dependent on men and who committed themselves to their own sex through the women's rights movement—were portrayed by Henry James in *The Bostonians* as fanatically driven, unfulfilled, and incomplete women. Freud offered the world a clinical diagnosis to explain single women who lived as Anthony did: Their choice was labeled sexual repression or sublimation of sex into work. By the turn of the century, the woman who refused to be dominated was seen by sexologists as cold and hard. In Anthony's case, her passionate charisma was reduced to evidence of rigid authoritarianism.

This letter, typical of Stanton's humor, also reflected her submission to romantic essentialism. She knew that an account of her best friend's love life would have justified Antony's work and her political life. Later in her own life, even Anthony herself succumbed to presenting the public with an identity which was not actually her own. Several times when questioned by reporters on the subject of her love life, she said that she had been in love many times, and quickly restored her story to her own reality by turning it into a political statement, saying that marriage without equality was inconceivable to her, and that she had never met an equal to marry. But in the effort to prove that she was normal and not sick or aberrant, she would overstate the being-in-love-several-times story (which was actually a relatively insignificant reality in her life). Whether or not this gave her ego satisfaction, it was something she eventually understood as necessary in order to get people to listen to her and to take seriously her political demands.

Patriarchal society will not accept any woman who refuses to be dominated. If she persists thus, it rewrites her history and reshapes her character, punitively twisting her will, bending her image, and distorting her identity; her defiance appears as a deformity—an aberration of nature. But over time it has proven impossible to completely suppress the reality of the lives of independent, self-defined women such as Susan B. Anthony. They periodically reemerge from behind the historical deformation of their lives to defy patriarchy once again. In traditional history, a life like Anthony's seems to be an anomaly; but to feminists, the anomaly suggests that her kind of life story actually says something about *all* women. In feminist research, the anomaly—the "rupture of history"—is often the point where we begin to look for women's reality. It is there that we comprehend the fuller extent of what patriarchy has distorted or excluded in its domination of women (Culture et pouvoir, Mars-Avril).

Like any other oppressed group, women live in the contradiction of actively and creatively constructing their own identity while the male-dominated society imposes a reductive, biologized identity upon them, thus remaking them into merely the products of drives and instincts. To the extent that women's lives do not fit the traditional female definitions, all women are misfits. For the past two decades the study of women's history and feminist theory has generated new research and insights that have begun to correct masculinized history. We have now reached a critical juncture where history and theory require grounding in women's realities. Women's biography is emerging as a new genre, which can challenge the very structure and categories of the history men have jealously guarded as their own.

Historical sociologists are beginning to unthink the dualisms in which macro has been disconnected from micro and the individual has been dissociated from theories of society. French philosopher Paul Ricoeur (1984) has criticized top-down history for replacing "the subjects of action with entities that are anonymous" (p. 177) and for making history a science that studies nations, societies, social classes, or mentalities. Feminist historians have broken ground by demonstrating the discontinuity between women's history and traditional historical periodization (Joan Kelly, 1984). By unpeopling history and sociology, and disconnecting daily life and subjective reality from the epochs, periods, and major social categories, grand history and macro-sociology have remained the strongholds of patriarchal thought. These disciplines are concerned with the history of the great wars, the grand philosophical traditions, the stories of great men, and the origins of theories. Against this male control of history women have recaptured their history—a new social history "from the bottom up." But that social history of women has not yet seriously impinged on or forced a reformulation of historical periodization, the epochs through which we have come to know the world.

Biography requires that we be true to our subject, that we not only recreate the phenomenology of daily life to uncover the subjectivity of the self, but that we locate our subject in her own historical context and that requires historical reperiodization. Thus biography can render the constructed divisions—which separate social history from grand history, divorce theory from reality, macro from micro—into false categorizations (see Sartre, 1981, for both biography and method that approaches the unity of these dichotomies). The theory of women's biography I have been developing since completing Susan B. Anthony's life story moves in a progression from the phenomenology of daily life to the structure of history. This theory is meant to force the anomalies, distortions, and eclipses of masculinized history into a new clarity. This is the beginning of a new study but I have chosen to develop some of the ideas here as they have originated in my study of Anthony's life.

History is key to the structuring of human subjectivity as it offers a past from which we can locate ourselves in time, culture, and community. When women are defined in terms of essentialist roles that are drawn from instinctual or biological mandates, they are confined to a personal past and known only through private existence. I am posing a very clear opposition between imposed essentialist determinism, that defines the female, and active social construction of woman in the world. I am intentionally situating these as polar opposites to create ideal types that crystallize the fullest reality at each end of the spectrum of identity, realizing that all that is between them is more complicated and confused than the oppositions themselves represent.

DISCOVERING THE ACTING SUBJECT

Feminists now must look at history with a new eye: the eye of a woman from her own historical group, the collective base of networks from which women come to be known as acting subjects of history. By history we mean subjective history. Our documents are women's lives: their letters, diaries, testimony, experiences, and interactions.

Subjective history begins with the life story. This is what Ricoeur (1984) refers to as a return to the narrative. He argues that "history cannot . . . sever every connection with narrative without losing its historical character" (p. 177). However, the narrative of life history must begin by garnering the facts and recreating the objective conditions of an individual's life. That is where I began with Susan B. Anthony's life. I began by reading all her diaries, papers, and letters, and even many of the books in her personal library, which is now in the Library of Congress. I followed her through exciting events and, likewise, lived through the mundane day-to-day routine: the repetitiveness that was reflected in many letters and diaries. Then as I read the statements from the women's rights movement, their conference calls and documents, articles from newspapers that covered their actions and Anthony's appearance in one city after another, she became more present to me, despite the century difference in our lives. I read her favorite novels, the ones most popular with women of her day, especially novelists and poets like Charlotte Brontë and Elizabeth Barrett Browning. I finally perceived from her reading of these novels what inspired her and what in them reflected her own life to her; this brought her even closer to me. Then I visited the villages and cities where she lived, spending afternoons walking down country roads and into city backyards to see what she saw. And while I was writing about her political work and sometimes finding her too distant from me, I even stood up, set up something like a lectern on my work table, and read some of her speeches aloud, as if they were being presented to audiences. I finally got a feel for her, a sense of who she was that went far beyond a studied analysis of her life. This was a different way of knowing that made her very present to me.

But up to that point of research, biographical study is only descriptive and because it does not go beyond description to interpretation of intention it is not yet connected to human subjectivity—that is, the self, the life force. The research has established the historical context from which biography grows from narrative into interpretation. Anthony would have remained a distant object, a model with whom I identified but did not know, until I went one step further and began to interpret the facts of her life by deriving the actual meaning she attributed to those facts. The research into her papers and documents allowed me to reconstruct the objective conditions of situations in Anthony's life. From them I was able to interpret the meanings that she attributed to her interactions both with herself and with others.

When we engage in this kind of interpretation with our biographical subject we necessarily interact with that individual. We begin to know our subject the way we know others in our lives. From that kind of knowing, we hope to be able to approximate how our subject knew herself and others in her life. As Anthony interpreted the words and gestures of those in her life, I found that the more fully I approximated her meaning in interpreting her words and actions, the more fully she became a subject to me because I was involved with her. As I began to apprehend Anthony's interactions with others, such as her family, her friends, and her foes and colleagues, I came to know her in a way that actually developed over time into a relationship with her. She was no longer the object of my study, she had become a subject to me. When that happened, true biographical work began.

But how can a biographer be sure of her interpretation of the meaning of the other when the other is not present to verify it? Sociologists usually rely on large numbers of subjects to reveal the patterns of social behavior because they can be treated as representative. It must be different with biography. As I progressed in my involvement with Anthony as a subject, I began to find myself almost automatically predicting her response or her course of action in particular situations; from the information in her letters or other documents, she would verify my interpretations. This is what sociologists call saturation when studying collective life histories; it is the point that one reaches when a certain predictability intervenes and becomes verified (Bertaux, 1980; Blumer, 1975).

Once this has happened, the relationship with the subject has passed beyond the basic level of interpretation just described and assumes a subjective connection as we do with close friends. We presume something because our interactions have taken us in closer, to a deeper level of knowing—that of subject to subject, or intersubjectivity. This is how I came to know Susan B. Anthony. At first there was an initial attraction and an interest in getting to know her better. It was not an instant knowledge or liking but one that developed over time and created closeness. For in involving ourselves in women's lives and touching their subjectivity, we begin to know what will ring true for them. This gave me a truly objective and dialectical point of reference to challenge the traditional historical interpretations of Anthony's life.

I summarized this dynamic of subjective interaction in a 1986 paper I delivered in Paris (see also Herbert Blumer 1969; George Herbert Mead, 1967)

> We are concerned here with the subjectivity of self as the self comes to be known to itself through interaction with others and with oneself where the interaction involves interpreting and internalizing the meaning of the other who then does not remain an object but becomes a subject to the self, a subject as the subjectivity in the interaction emerges and is internalized by the other. This is not only the basis for interpreting biography, but it forms the core of social life, it creates the connections among individuals, the means by which we are located in the social world. One's subjectivity, however, can never be fully or completely comprehended or interpreted by the other; nor should we want to for it is in the fullness of my own subjectivity that I am the "me" who is distinguished from others, this is where we know the unique in ourselves. (Kathleen Barry, 1986)

Finding and revealing a woman's subjectivity should not be confused with identifying with her. Many biographers today talk about their identification with their subject to the extent that it is sometimes assumed that to write a biography is to write one's own autobiography. I disagree. It is true that women like Susan B. Anthony and Elizabeth Cady Stanton remain important models for women of today. Many women have identified with them, likened our struggle to theirs, and have taken courage from their spirited lives. But the biographer must take a further step and transcend personal identification with her subject. If, as the biographer of Susan B. Anthony, I identified with her, and found my life in her biography, I would have falsely equated us. Ultimately, identification is not an equation at all but a kind of heroine worship; it is an objectification of the other—a refusal of subjectivity, a denial that intersubjective interaction is possible. Instead of identification, I came to share a dialectical relationship with Anthony that continually revealed more to me about how she knew herself and how she knew and interacted with others. Surprisingly, I came to know more of myself through my interaction with her.

Subjectivity, the necessary but insufficient condition of women's biography, also requires historical context—that dimension which makes it possible to reveal the acting subject in movement over time. Probably the most important impact of essentialist determinism in the (de)formation of human subjectivity is in how it shapes temporality. To define women by their sexuality and reproductivity is to remove them from the progression of history. In contrast to the historical understanding of women as acting subjects of history, through essentialism women are universalized by sexual relations and/or motherhood. Without a concrete location in history, there is no social cohesion to bind woman to woman. Likewise without a group identity, women are made more vulnerable to being reduced to the ahistorical. This is where essentialism enters and makes women socially atomized. Woman, alone with her husband, lover, or family, is isolated from the social realities that would bond her with her sex. Essentialism as such constitutes an effort to annihilate women's subjectivity. It is a lie about one's self. It is a lie about women, because it rests on the assumption that one's self is unrelated to other similar selves. To not be able to identify oneself with a "we" is to not take one's group or oneself as subjects of history.

Susan B. Anthony's biography is the story of a single woman who constructed her life course by surpassing the impositions of biological determinisms on her identity, while the social rejection she experienced for nonidentity with women's role revealed the regulatory force it held over women as a class. Because she was single and thus able to sustain an unbroken identity with her sex her biography reveals that woman in marriage is not able to be a woman unto herself and therefore she is isolated from other women leaving her to construct her primary identity through her husband and in her family. Marriage and any form of relationship which causes women to shift their identity from themselves separates women from each other, denies them their identity with their own sex—their class of women—that thereby denies them a true sense of we. For Anthony, being single—that is, a woman unto herself—no longer meant being alone and separate. Her life story reveals that, for her, being single meant affirming her identity as a woman with women. In other words, she did not have to become unsingle. She did not have to change her name, her legal status, or shift her needs and identity from herself and her woman's world to a mate, as did her married sisters. For Susan B. Anthony, being single meant that she identified herself with a woman's *we,* a yet unrecognized social reality. Because she was not married she was able to live in, with, and through her own group—women. This unbroken identity eventually led her to the center of the women's movement, where her political identification with her own group was built not only in reaction to being oppressed but also from the independence of women coming together out of their own strength. In this way, women transcend the alienation of the self—which becomes locked into essentialist meanings—by actively pursuing their own lives in a social context that does not prohibit group identification. The social construction of self that refuses to be determined by natural, inevitable roles provides the beginning point for exploring who women are as a class, and will ultimately direct us to locate women in their valid historical context.

Not being particularly interested in marriage and ultimately refusing the role of the old maid, Anthony faced the world with few models before her. At that moment she began to make choices. Even though she was not sure what she would do or where it would take her, she discovered a new sense of the future that opened up before her. Her seemingly ordinary choices—such as deciding to spend more time working for temperance reform than in her garden which she loved—were relentlessly moving her into directions women had not taken before.

Unmarked by ceremony, gifts, and congratulations, the choice to be single is usually found in small acts, seemingly insignificant decisions that move one in immediately imperceptible ways away from marriage—sometimes even before one has rejected marriage per se. It may not be so much reaction against marriage more than it is a disinterest in this social institution. Being single involves no dramatic breaks, no severing or disruption of one's identity.

Making choices moved Anthony out of her cousin's family. It broke her away from women's private sphere. But when I followed her from the private sphere to the public world, it became apparent that merely having an independent will and income was not enough to prepare her for the world outside of the home and teaching.

True womanhood—with its personal, moralistic piety—was seen as not only appropriate for women's morality but for rearing children (which is why teaching was so compatible with women's private sphere). Women had internalized the Puritan morality that caused them to understand the character of morality as individual and self-searching; morality was signified by the transgression of God's will and rectified by a personal piety that led to righteousness over private behaviors. Women monitored themselves, each other, and their children. Confined to an individual level, this moralistic piety became for many women a way of not knowing the world outside the family—their private sphere. When Anthony began her political work, the woman's movement was evoking a different historical context. Her moral piety shifted while her moral precepts did not.

This change from home to society—from private moralistic piety to public, group-orientated moral analysis of issues in ethical terms fit for public discourse—was not only a personal shift for Susan B. Anthony. Her individual experience at this time was mirrored by the women's movement in general. I agree with the feminist historians who credit the women who participated in temperance reform work in the 1840s with the real beginnings of the 19th-century American women's rights movement. But further distinctions must be made between the two movements of women's protest. The first phase associated with early temperance work was preconscious feminism. Temperance reform focused on individuals and on personal solutions to private behavior that would remain private. The reformers thought neither of changing society nor of analyzing the problem beyond its individual manifestations. Their approach was: If liquor makes men drunk and drunk men are abusive then take the liquor away from them. Women could speak in public but from a personal morality meant only for the private sphere. In many ways, this assured their opponents that their threats and acts were ultimately harmless. With the Declaration of Sentiments, written by Elizabeth Cady Stanton and adopted at the 1848 Seneca Falls convention, privatized morality was transformed into political issues that confronted the civil and legal structures supporting the patriarchal domination of women.

Personal transformation of morality involves restructuring women's subjectivity. In 1852, as president of Anthony's newly formed Woman's State Temperance Society, Stanton declared:

> Let no woman remain in the relation of wife with a confirmed drunkard. Let no drunkard be the father of her children. . . . Let us petition our State government so to modify the laws affecting marriage and the custody of children, that the drunkard shall have no claims on wife or child. (Barry, 1989, 367)

When Anthony's morality was transformed to the public sphere, she reversed social causality. She showed that it was not alcohol that threatens women and the family, but the structure of marriage that makes women vulnerable to drunken husbands. Her new analysis reflected a shift in emphasis to society, group behavior, institutions, and political meanings. Her private righteousness over personal transgression became externalized to a civil responsibility and an egalitarian ethic fit for confronting social issues in the public world. Anthony learned that it was not women's private, moralistic piety that allowed women to influence the world as the guardians of its morality. It was actually the reverse: The public sphere, controlled by men, defined the limits and shaped the possibilities of the private.

As Anthony's subjectivity reformed around her egalitarian ethics, her political work took on clear definition. A violation of the moral code was no longer wrong because it offended some value precepts of propriety or ideas of personal sinfulness, but because it violated human beings' civil and political rights. Further, that violation was found not only in individual acts, it was systematized into institutions—like marriage and slavery—and legalized by the courts and governments. Transformation from internalized piety to moral and ethical positions taken in the public world was a struggle in political consciousness, a story of the reformulation of subjectivity that became necessary once Anthony began to make choices that took her outside the home and teaching.

What I am developing is a theory of women's subjectivity and political consciousness that identifies development as transformation and not merely a progression from one stage to another. Political consciousness is consciousness of domination and it requires unlearning the lesson that one has been taught so one will no longer "know" that one and one's group are the objects of domination. Under domination, morality is internalized and shapes the self so that one will not conflict with or challenge power. In the 19th century, this meant adhering to a morality that was not intended to go beyond the private sphere. To take moral and ethical positions over their demands for legal and political rights, women and their movement had to transform their morality into an ethical responsibility that would reflect both their analysis of collective domination and the moral bases for their proposed remedies. In Anthony's case, this meant abandoning the piety of true womanhood for a morality based on radical egalitarianism.

The effect of Anthony was pronounced and it reveals how political consciousness shapes subjectivity. Consciousness of domination produced awareness of the possibilities which would surpass it. As Anthony's public work opened new futures to her with many unknowns before her, her life began to reveal what had happened to women like her married sisters whose lives were defined by impossibilities rather than opportunities. Marriage revealed what women cannot, must not, should not, and ultimately will not do. Anthony transformed the objective reality of an old maid's life into a new reality for herself, which surpassed the previous definition of women, and the future opened before her. Sartre's (1968) concept of "the negation of the negation" is useful here. He shows that "defined by the negation of the refused reality in the name of the reality to be produced, it remains the captive of the action which it clarifies, and disappears along with it," (p. 92) and that "only the project, as a mediation between two moments of objectivity can account for history; that is for human creativity" (p. 99).

By transforming personal piety into civil responsibility, she began to connect her experience of choice and possibility to all women and to the objective conditions that block their future, as well as to the conditions that transcend their immanence—which domination makes impossible. (See Simone de Beauvoir [1953], where she equates immanence with stagnation, "the brutish life of subjection to given conditions.") This revealing knowledge of the self and the other is *political consciousness*.

The fulcrum between the individual and history is the social group. In 1949, Simone de Beauvoir noted that except in feminist gatherings, women do not say "we;" by contrast, "Proletarians say 'We;' Negroes also. Regarding themselves as subjects, they transform the bourgeois, the whites, into 'others.' But women do not say we" (de Beauvoir, 1953, xxviii). And that makes it impossible to effectively confront domination because women cannot enter history one by one. Whether or not any one woman overtly identifies with women as her group, women exist as a class by virtue of their collective relations to male power. To claim their own history, women must be located in their own historical group.

How then do women form their own group identity? What is involved in restructuring subjectivity from being unsingle to identification with oneself and with women. Determinisms are overcome through choice. Making choices and projecting from the past onto a new activity means realizing not only what one *can* do but what one *must* do. This continually reveals new possibilities—new becoming (Jean Paul Sartre, 1963/1968, pp. 85–100). Again Anthony's life is illustrative. As I indicated in her biography, the decision to remain single is socially (that is, politically) interpreted as an inevitability or nonchoice. Deciding to marry is given the appearance of a dramatic decision marked by legal announcements, civil and religious ceremonies, change of residence, and for the woman change of social status. In other words, marriage appears to be the institution that is socially constructed and chosen—therefore not at all inevitable. Yet the social pressure for women to be married encloses women in atemporal, universalized roles of sexuality and motherhood, the active context in which domination is internalized and the inevitability associated with those roles becomes subjectively structured into the marital dyads and dissociates women from their class identity. The ontological loneliness of being unsingle, when identity is formed around and through someone other than one's self, is the consequence of marriage breaking women away from their identity with their subjective we.

In opposition to this world view of woman stands woman's dream to be a woman unto herself. To be a woman whose identity and life are shaped through her ideas, her actions, and her own projects. The desire to live with another and, contradictorily, to be a woman unto herself is more of a dilemma for many late 20th-century women than it was for our sisters a century before. Some women attempt to approximate that dream by finding "a room of one's own." Others realize some of what it means to be a woman unto oneself when their children are grown and gone, and they are no longer with their mate. Tragically, some women never touch these possibilities. Indeed, in our times, it is the intention of right-wing antifeminism to insure that women never will.

BIOGRAPHY AS HISTORY

From examining women's lives, we can redefine the meaning of being a woman and discover what masculine history has suppressed: how women make history and therefore who women are. Thus, women's biography must be a new reading of history, which demands the rewriting of all history. But that is not enough. Women's lives have either been hidden behind portrayals of them as wives, mothers, and lovers; or, when women cannot be defined through essentialist images, their lives have been viciously distorted, as in the case of Susan B. Anthony.

Too often biographies of women have short-changed their subjects by assuming that the fullness of women's subjectivity is equatable with their personal lives—where intimate relationships with husbands, lovers, and children often usurp the search for interaction and subjectivity that we discover when we find the diverse and significant ways women act in their own historical circumstances. The emerging genre of women's biography must be based on a search for women's subjectivity, where the subject becomes known to us through her actions and her history. History becomes a dynamic active force revealed in the present, acting on the future. Therefore this concept of women's biography cannot be concerned with "placing women in history"—as if history is an already formed reality and all we need to do is make a slot in it for women.

Here we must distinguish between the interpretation necessary in women's biography from that in biographies of men. Generally men's life stories reflect the known society and accepted renditions of history. Consequently traditional historical periodization provides a valid base for interpreting men's lives because it highlights and reveals them. But women's biography must break through the essentialisms that have a grasp on their identities and give them their place in society. In lifting women's biography from its imbeddedness in essentialism, women's history can be found through biographical interpretation; this enters into the historical complexity and multidimensionality of women's lives that has been made all the more complex by their exclusion from history. If women's biography is written from an approach that begins with their roles as mothers and sexual partners, where a history of childbearing and motherhood is simply added on, the result is that women's lives are not treated as if they are multidimensional at all. They remain detached from the grand epochs and periods of history.

In writing the biography of Susan B. Anthony, I was able to discover her as an acting subject by exploring the choices she made—the large and small ones, as well as the significant and insignificant ones. Choice is action; it reveals human engagement with the world and others around us. It is the social plane where one interacts from intentionality with received reality. Making choices moves the individual from receiving reality to acting upon it and thus translating received reality into her life. Choice has to do with the future; it is constantly renewed forward motion toward something. The future and how a woman interacts with it are shaped by and require projecting from the past.

These distinctions are critical to understanding how women internalize domination, because the ability to conceptualize the future, and the history from which the future is projected, are crucial to experiencing and learning who we are and what we can become. If woman is limited to a personal past, which detaches her from identification with her group, and if history has excluded or diminished the representation of her group in its story, her subjectivity becomes structured by a past and therefore a future that is confined by these limits. A confined and limited future diminishes possibility and that in turn will effect how far a woman thinks she can go in acting for and from herself. In that case, when a woman projects beyond her personal life, she faces only a history of the "other:" He is historical, and he understands her as a timeless universal. Her subjectivity, confined to the personal, is limited, defined, and deformed by a temporality and universalization which have been her bases for formulating her future. In contrast, women's biography that is engaged with the subjects in her multidimensionality restores a history to women that breaks their atemporality.

Therefore, women's biography can no longer be confined to the story of women's private lives. Nor can women be satisfied only with a rich, new social history of everyday life, even though these accounts have given us histories of the hidden realities of housework, motherhood, and of women's networks. It takes women organized on their own behalf to reclaim all that men have appropriated for themselves—particularly the grand periods, major epochs, and eras of their history. Women's history will be a comprehensive reality when not only are the stories of individual women and the histories of women's daily lives recorded but when feminism forces a rewriting of all history. Through biography we well come to know who woman is and what she can be—even by facing what she has been denied, not permitted, or forbidden to own of herself and the world. Recapturing biography for women is to insist on having it all for our subject, for her class, and for ourselves.

REFERENCES

Barry, Kathleen. (1986). The method of biography in feminist research. Paper presented at Centre Nationale de la Recherche Scientifique, Laboratoire d'Anthropologie Sociale, Paris.

Bertaux, Daniel. (1980). L'approche biographique, sa validite methodologique, ses potentialitiés [the biographical approach, its methodological validity, its potentials]. *Cahiers Internationaux de Sociologie, 69,* 206–208.

Blumer, Herbert. (1975). Introduction to the transaction edition. Critique of research in the social sciences, an appraisal of Thomas and Zaniescki's "The Polish *Peasant in America*" (pp. xxx–xxxiii). New Brunswick: Transaction.

Culture et pouvoir des femmes: Essai d'historiographie [Culture and power of women: Attempt at a historiography]. Centre des recherches historique, *Annales,* Mars-Avril, 2, 290.

de Beauvoir, Simone. (1953). *The second sex* (p. xviii). Translated from the French by H. M. Parshley. New York: Bantam.

James, Henry. (1976). *The Bostonians.* (A. Habegger, Ed.) Indianapolis: Bobbs-Merrill.

Kelly, Joan. (1984). The social relation of the sexes: Methodological implications of women's history. In Joan Kelly (Ed.), *Women, history and theory.* Chicago: University of Chicago Press.

Ricoeur, Paul. (1984). *Time and narrative* (Vol. 1, p. 177). Translated by Kathleen McLaughlin and David Pellauer. Chicago: University of Chicago Press.

Sartre, Jean Paul. (1968). *The search for a method* (pp. 85–100). New York: Vintage.

Sartre, Jean Paul. (1981). *The family idiot: Gustave Flaubert, 1821–1857, Vol 1* (Carol Cosman, Trans.). Chicago: University of Chicago Press.

Stanton, Theodore, & Stanton Blatch, Harriot. (1922). *Elizabeth Cady Stanton as revealed in her letters, diary, and reminiscences* (Vol. 1). New York: Harper.

Chapter 4

Are You Writing Fact or Fiction?

Pilar Hidalgo

The idea that a text has an infinite variety of meanings has become a critical commonplace; that infinity, though, is not generated from within, but from the questions we as readers bring to it. I intend to suggest here that we can approach women writers' biographies as we would women's fiction, that we can seek to elicit from biographical texts some of the answers we could find relevant in women's fiction.

By tracing the connections between women's biography and women's fiction, and by focusing on writers who came of age at a time of heightened feminist consciousness, I will explore the different (or not so different) ways in which the lives and works of Rebecca West, Vita Sackville-West, and Virginia Woolf illuminate basic feminist issues. I will address to what extent the feminist is found in their lives and their fiction, and what can be said about the relation. I have structured the fictional and biographical material along the lines of thematics, imagery, authorial point of view, and narrative endings, and have chosen to highlight some specific points: Vita's Sackville-West's love for Knole and her sense of dispossession, Rebecca West's relationship with H. G. Wells, and Virginia Woolf's exorcism of her past in *To the Lighthouse* (1927).

The structural and thematic aspects that fiction and biography share lead to an analysis of whether works of fiction by the subject of a biography can add to our understanding of a given life, and vice versa. The question of bias in a writer's attitude towards his or her characters is best seen in particular cases, such as West's travesty of her elder sister in *The Fountain Overflow* (1957/1984) and her idealization of her father in the same novel. The way a biographer valorizes or dismisses a particular aspect of his or her subject's life and work gives us an insight into the sort of "character" he or she is creating. The treatment Virginia Woolf receives at the hands of three biographers (specifically through their accounts of *To the Lighthouse* and *Three Guineas,* and also their accounts of her death) provides the opportunity for further discussion of the problems of women's creativity in a man-dominated world.

THEME

Vita Sackville-West

I begin with a thematic approach, looking at the writing of Vita Sackville-West and Rebecca West, both of whom have been biographical subjects for Victoria Glendinning. In the biography of Vita, whose aristocratic background is always a part of the picture, Glendinning (1983/1984) does incorporate explicitly feminist moments, most of which occur, significantly enough, in Vita's arguments with her husband, Harold Nicholson. Glendinning quotes from an entry made in Harold's diary on February 23, 1934 which records a conversation with Vita in Casablanca on the subject of women's freedom. Harold expresses the view that equality between the sexes is impossible, and that woman's "proper function" is only fulfilled in subservience to some man (Glendinning, 1983/1986, p. 270). He adds that he did not communicate his opinions to Vita in order not to hurt her feelings. Harold's diary for September 30, 1933, also mentions "a discussion about women's rights" with Vita, but does not elaborate (p. 267). Vita herself refutes Nicolson's assumptions about the inferiority of women in a letter quoted in the biography (p. 199); Glendinning, who rarely privileges a feminist reading of her subject, nevertheless comments on Vita's denials of becoming a feminist: "her very attitude—to domestic life, to her work, to the bureaucracy that insisted on labelling her Mrs. Harold Nicolson—belied her" (p. 201).

Just as Vita Sackville-West fictionalized her deep emotional and aesthetic response to Knole in *The Edwardians* (1930), and her love affair with Violet Trefusis in *The Challenge* (1920), *All Passion Spent* (1931) is her most powerful feminist statement. Exploring the fate of the woman artist in a patriarchal society, *All Passion Spent* has deep affinities with Woolf's *To the Lighthouse, A Room of One's Own* (1928), and *Between the Acts* (1941), although—unlike Lily Briscoe or Miss La Trobe—Lady Slane, the 88-year-old protagonist, had forsaken her aspiration to be a painter when she married. The presentation of thwarted female talent has, of course, a long tradition in the English novel; what is striking about *All Passion Spent* is the thorough critique of male values and hierarchies.

Lady Slane's recollections of her life as the wife of a former Viceroy of India and British Prime Minister offer, in an impressionistic manner, telling glimpses of patriarchal attitudes to women; they also echo the crucial point Woolf had made in *To the Lighthouse* about men's draining of their wives' emotional energy with their constant need for reassurance:

> And when she had accomplished this feat, this reconstruction of extreme delicacy and extreme solidity—when he left her, to go back strengthened to his business—then with her hands lying limp, symbol of her exhaustion, and a sweet emptiness within her, as though her self had drained away to flow into the veins of another person—then, sinking, drowning, she wondered whether she had not secretly touched the heights of rapture. (Sackville-West, 1931/1983, pp. 173–174)

The Woolfian connection becomes more evident when we juxtapose Vita's fictional account of Lady Slane's subservience to her husband with Phyllis Rose's comment on Leslie Stephen's demand of female service from his daughters after his wife Julia had died:

> This 'legacy of dependence' survived Julia and became a terrible burden for her daughters—one of whom, at least, couldn't help noticing that Julia, so concerned about her husband's health, had died of fatigue at forty-nine while cancer found it very hard to kill Sir Leslie at seventy-two. (Rose, 1978/1986, pp. 18–19)

Lady Slane's story embodies two classic feminist themes: the thwarting of women's abilities and talent, and male exploitation of women's emotional reserves. More unexpected is the presentation of Lady Slane's experience during the weeks preceding her wedding. Although she and her husband seem to have been sexually compatible, she experiences something of the same rage at the way young girls are kept in ignorance about sexual matters that George Egerton had expressed almost 40 years before in her short story "Virgin Soil" (1894). The sense of impending violation conveyed by Egerton's description of the newlyweds' departure on their honeymoon—

> The bell rings, the guard locks the door, the train steams out, and as it passes the signal-box, a large well-kept hand, with a signet ring on the little finger, pulls down the blind on the window of an engaged carriage. (Egerton, 1894/1987, p. 192)

—has a parallel in the image of virgin sacrifice that Sackville-West puts in Deborah's mind as she is about to marry Henry Slane: "Yet he was there, terribly there, in the background; and thus, she thought, might a Theban mother have tired her daughter before sending her off to the Minotaur" (p. 158).

Rebecca West

Born in the same year as Vita, Rebecca West belongs thus to the generation of women writers who came of age in the years of the suffrage campaign. Unlike Vita, Rebecca West was actively committed to the feminist cause and, as a journalist, published extensively on feminist issues. Nonetheless, and as far as her fiction is concerned, it is more difficult to find a clear-cut feminist statement, such as Vita's in *All Passion Spent.* As Claire Tylee (1988) points out about West's first novel, *The Return of the Soldier* (1918):

> There is no indication in the novel that women might find some purpose to their lives apart from domesticity. No indication that there might exist those adventurous-minded young women of whom West wrote in 1912, that they might, for instance, wish to be wireless operators on board ship in order "to see over the edge of the world." In fact the novel even presents a justification for the "parasitic women" of Kitty's class that West had so objected to before the war" (p. 190)

Although West also fictionalized the question of the woman artist in *Harriet Hume* (1928), she didn't dwell on patriarchal restrictions on women's creativity, as both Sackville-West and Woolf had done, but rather explored her favorite theme of the polarization between female and male values. It is true that in charting the political career of Arnold Condorex as a chain of betrayal, expediency, and ultimately corruption, West exposes patriarchal values along lines similar to those of Woolf in *Mrs. Dalloway* and *Three Guineas,* or Sackville-West in *All Passion Spent.* But in the end she cannot resist the fatal attraction of a fairy-tale reconciliation, driven perhaps by her yearning for that world "where men are still men and women still women" which she would eventually believe to have found in Dalmatia (Glendinning, 1987, p. 156).

It is Rebecca West's life rather than her novels that provides the material for a feminist analysis. Of course some of her articles for *The Freewoman, The New Freewoman,* and *The Clarion,* which Jane Marcus has made available for present-day readers (Marcus, 1982), are among the classic polemical texts of 20th-century British feminism. Furthermore, her early story "Indissoluble Matrimony" (1914) has been read as a percipient fictional rendering of male sexual anxiety in the face of women's growing autonomy; for Sandra Gilbert and Susan Gubar (1988) "the tale marks a key moment in the female story of sexual battle, a moment when the woman is seen as unequivocally victorious" (p. 100).

From a biographical point of view, feminist explorations of West have focused on her relationship with H. G. Wells. This is not so surprising as it may seem. West herself saw her relationship with Wells as one of the central events in her life. Also, the love affair of an independent-minded, brilliant young woman with a world-famous, middle-aged writer encompassed some basic issues in sexual politics. The fact that Wells had already written his so-called "feminist" novels (*Ann Veronica,* 1909; *The New Machiavelli,* 1911) when he met Rebecca West makes their relationship all the more significant.

In her biography of Rebecca West, Victoria Glendinning (1987) has divided her subject's long life into six parts, according to the different names by which she was known. West was born Cicely Fairfield, took Rebecca West as her *nom de plume,* and became Mrs. Henry Andrews when she married. The second part is called "Panther," the pet name Wells gave her (he was "Jaguar"). Soon after she starts telling the story of the love affair, Glendinning has to come to terms with the contradictions between Wells's public and private attitudes:

> Wells called himself a feminist, but repeatedly made fun of the militants for their political ignorance, weak arguments and—worst sin of all, where he was concerned—their physical unattractiveness. Wells found it impossible to think of women except in their relation to men, and considered "independent women" ridiculous and pathetic. The freedom he wanted from them was sexual freedom, which meant in practice sexual availability. (Glendinning, 1987, p. 48)

Besides highlighting the ingrained conservatism held toward women by supposedly progressive men—a familiar story by now—Glendinning's narrative foregrounds key female issues: women's lack of control over their bodies (West's baby was not intended), the plight of the single mother as a result of the double standard (mitigated in West's case by the fact that she received economic support from Wells and, moving as she did in bohemian and intellectual circles, was not so dependent on societal approval), and finally, men's exploitative dependence on women for bodily comforts and emotional reassurance.

Like his fictional counterparts Mr. Ramsay and Henry Slane, H. G. Wells expected women to minister to his needs; with what Glendinning calls his "sublime selfishness" (p. 65), he complained about being "encumbered" with his little boy, whom of course he only saw when he visited Rebecca. It would be wrong to ignore the extent to which West herself accepted the situation because she was in love with the man; not for the first (or last) time, a strong, self-aware woman ran into private/political difficulties over a choice of a male partner. It would also certainly be wrong not to be aware that her choices—if she wanted a man—were limited: where would she find such a one who would engage with her on equal and honorable terms?

Whereas in Glendinning's (1987) full-length biography the West/Wells love affair is just one part among six others, Fay Weldon (1985) chose to focus her brief biographical account on the days before and after Rebecca bore Wells's child. Weldon's story also has the peculiarity of being in the second person, a form of narrative as rare in biography as it is in fiction. Biography, like history and the classical novel, is particularly well-suited to third-person narration, and Weldon's use of the second person makes the story she has to tell all the more immediate. Significantly, Victoria Glendinning began her third-person biography of West with a first-person vignette.

To anyone familiar with Fay Weldon's fiction, it comes as no surprise that she could start her account at the very moment when Rebecca is about to give birth to her son, Anthony. Women's biological functions figure prominently in her novels, from the pitfalls of going into labor during a public holiday—when hospital staff will be unavailable or drunk *(Down Among the Women, Female Friends)*—to the gynecological treatise embedded in *Puffball*. As an unmarried woman in labor and a writer, Rebecca West in 1914 embodied some basic feminist issues which Weldon does not waste time in laying bare; these included male bullying:

> "You did keep the work going for a while, but then H. G. said (jokingly) that it was bad for the unborn baby, it would soften its bones" (Fay Welson, 1985; p. 29);

and general unhelpfulness:

> "H. G. can't abide illness" (p. 29);

plus hostility from men writers:

> "Not only because you are a suffragist and want to be allowed to vote, and govern countries, but because you are a critic, an essayist and a reviewer and are taking the bread out of their mouths" (p. 33).

FICTION AND NONFICTION

So far I have explored the connections between women's biography and women's fiction from the point of view of thematics. Feminist perspectives on the relationship between biography and fiction could also be sought on the basis of the existence of value-laden images in any writer's rendering of reality, and hence in a biographer's account of a life. The distinction between fiction and nonfiction is especially unhelpful when applied to women's writing in the 20th century, because one of the most powerful recurrent images in the female novel—the room of one's own, signifying the freedom from being constantly available to the needs of others—comes of course from a work of nonfiction. Rooms have always played important metaphorical roles in women's novels: Fanny Price's cold room at Mansfield Park; the third-story room where Bertha Mason lurks in *Jane Eyre;* the two "hot, close rooms" where Lucy Snowe lives with Miss Marchmont in *Villette;* Rebekah's small room in Olive Schreiner's *From Man to Man,* which Elaine Showalter (1977) sees as "all too clearly and pathetically the embodiment of her femaleness" (p. 202); the red and black rooms in Doris Lessing; and so on. It is therefore ironical that when a woman writer uses a spacious, stately country house as the correlative of her imaginative powers, she should have done so out of a feeling of dispossession.

Vita Sackville-West

Although Vita Sackville-West's spectacular elopement with Violet Trefusis in 1920 may seem to some the central event in her life, I think that both her life and her fiction are best approached through the gates of Knole, the Kent country house where she was born. Glendinning begins her biography of Vita with a description of Knole; in her introduction to Vita's novel *The Edwardians,* she stresses the quasi-mythical value that the place had for Sackville-West:

> Her personal myth centred on Knole, the great house in Kent that had belonged to her ancestors since the reign of the first Queen Elizabeth . . . an only child, Vita had been brought up at Knole and loved it more, she often said, than she loved any human being except her husband. Because she was a woman, she was disqualified from inheriting Knole on the death of her father; the loss of Knole was the great grief of her life. (Glendinning, 1983, p. ix)

What Glendinning gives us at the start of her biography are the plain facts about Knole: There are said to be 52 staircases and 365 rooms in the house, the complex of stone buildings was built mainly in the 15th century and covers more than six acres, the main gates of the park open into the high street of Sevenoaks, and so on.

Vita's *The Edwardians* also opens with a description of Knole (called Chevron in the novel) seen from the roof where Sebastian had climbed. Sebastian being a male, he is the heir to Chevron, and although his view from the heights affords the reader a few glimpses of the house (the carvings of heraldic leopards, the courtyards, the deer in the park), Chevron/Knole functions in the novel not so much as an aesthetic object as a way of life. In the second chapter, after his mother's weekend guests have departed, Sebastian sees the life around him in terms of continuity, order, and community. Curiously enough, the emphasis is firmly placed on the human effort that keeps a place like Chevron/Knole going: grooming horses, hammering upon the anvil, chopping faggots, cooking, washing the linen, making jam, putting away the plate, and so on. Apart from the central role that Knole played in Vita's life and in her imagination, a sense of place would always be essential to her. Glendinning shows how Vita and her husband, from the beginning of their married life, successfully collaborated in creating an environment (Glendinning, 1983, p. 70); in *All Passion Spent,* Lady Slane's rejection of her late husband's values is symbolized by her moving to a house in Hampstead, where she can take possession of the room of her own that she had been denied 60 years before when she had married Henry Slane.

Rebecca West

While Vita Sackville-West's imagery is basically spatial, Rebecca West's language strikes the reader by the rich sensuousness of her perceptions. In place of Knole, music holds the infinite promise of life in West's novels:

Her fictional women artists (Harriet Hume and Rose Aubrey) are musicians. In her masterpiece, *The Fountain Overflows* (1957/1984), two statements stress the centrality of music for Rebecca in her own life. The first is made by Mrs. Aubrey to her daughter Rose: "You must always believe that life is as extraordinary as music says it is" (p. 210). The second is more surprising, coming as it does from Cordelia, the only daughter of Mrs. Aubrey who is musically untalented, although she tries very hard to be a good musician. To the question posed by odious Cousin Jock, "What's the good of music if there's all this cancer in the world?", Cordelia answers, "What's the harm in cancer, if there's all this music in the world?" (p. 305).

Rebecca West's prose style displays a marvellous alertness to sensuous detail which is especially evident in the presentation of food: "Here there were huge joints of beef, marbled with broad veins of fat, pork with splendid crackling, shining moulds of brawn and great tongues lolling back to themselves, golden-crusted pies, jewel-bright jellies, foaming syllabubs, pitchers of solid cream, cheeses big as millstones, of sorts not known today" (West, 1957/1984, p. 46). Besides actual descriptions similar to the one just quoted, food imagery is used to striking effect: "There was a golden heaviness about her face, to look on it was like watching honey drop slowly from a spoon" (p. 93). Or again, there is the delicate sensuality of the children's washing their hair, roasting chestnuts among the coals and eating them hot with milk that had been put outside the window to get very cold (p. 223).

Food imagery generally has positive, enjoyable connotations for Rebecca West, but there are some exceptions. For example, she used the same unpleasant simile in fiction and in real life to refer to Parliament. In *The Fountain Overflows,* Rose Aubrey accompanies her father on a visit to the House and sits with him in the central lobby: "It was like sitting in the midst of a tureen full of gravy soup" (p. 262). Glendinning reports the advice West gave to a friend of hers who wanted to get into Parliament: "I don't know why you want to get into the House, which seems to me like a brown earthenware soup tureen, filled with greasy oxtail soup" (Glendinning, 1987, p. 193). It is therefore fitting that, after having quoted Rebecca West on fresh and stale lobster as metaphor for the perception of the good and the bad in life, Glendinning (1987) should have resorted to a culinary metaphor: "Rebecca had lots of fresh lobster, figuratively and literally, in her long life" (p. 109).

Because both biography and fiction are narratives, it is relatively easy to perceive the connections in terms of thematics, imagery, and narrative structure. A relevant question is whether fiction can add to our understanding of biography, or whether it may just fudge the issues. A case in point is the fictional presentation of real-life characters. What does *Orlando* tell us about Virginia Woolf's feelings for Vita that we cannot find in the biographies of both writers, in Woolf's diaries, or in the letters they wrote to each other? An answer to this would necessarily and obviously depend on what the reader brings to the work. Biography tends to rely more on statement than fiction does; thus, Glendinning's (1987) assertions about Rebecca West's father, "Charles Fairfield was a romantic figure to his daughters" (p. 10) and "Cissie's picture of her father became with time a mixture of nostalgia and wish-fulfilment" (p. 17), are grounded not only on West's own pronouncements, but also on her presentation of her father in *The Fountain Overflows,* where Charles Fairfield/Piers Aubrey is shown indirectly through his effect on his family. The father's improvidence may come devastatingly upon the reader (but not upon his small daughter) when Mrs. Aubrey and Rose visit their Edinburgh flat in the first chapter of the novel and find that Aubrey has sold the family furniture.

The authorial voice in fiction sometimes offers corroboration of the writer's views expressed in nonfiction (letters, diaries, interviews, essays, etc.). Like Vita Sackville-West through Lady Slane and Virginia Woolf through Mrs. Ramsay, Rebecca West uses the narrator's voice in *The Return of the Soldier* to comment on a crucial aspect of women's emotional life:

> It means that the woman has gathered the soul of the man into her soul and is keeping it warm in love and peace so that his body can rest quiet for a little time. That is a great thing for a woman to do. (West, 1918/1987, pp. 143–4)

But perhaps the most illuminating aspect of the relationship between "real" life (and hence biography) and fiction lies in the presence of bias in the creation of character. West, who brilliantly discussed this side of novel-writing in *The Strange Necessity* (West, 1928/1931, pp. 90–121), travestied her sister Lettie in the figure of Cordelia, Rose Aubrey's elder sister in *The Fountain Overflows*. Obviously, Cordelia isn't "like" Letitia Fairfield, but reflects West's feelings towards her sister. As Glendinning (1987) points out, West filled many pages of notebooks and letters with diatribes against her elder sister: "Rebecca downgraded Lettie's impressive professional achievements, disliked hearing her praised and granted her no virtues—except, secretly, the most terrifying virtue of all, that of being in the right" (p. 54). In this way, *The Fountain Overflows* bears out the biographer's statements about her subject's attitude toward her sister. What is at issue is Rebecca West's subjective truth, not her sister's genuine personality. As West herself confessed, " 'I know I have largely invented my sister Lettie' " (Glendinning, 1987, p. 54).

The question of bias in a writer's attitude towards her characters comes also to the fore in a biographer's feelings toward her subject and toward the people who were important in her subject's life.

Virginia Woolf

Biographies of Virginia Woolf are extremely relevant on this point. If we look at biography as another author's "fiction" of a particular writer, it becomes obvious that different biographers of the same writer create distinct "characters" out of their subjects. The biographies of Woolf by Quentin Bell

(1973), Phyllis Rose (1978/1986), and Lyndall Gordon (1984/1986) signal their divergent approaches from the very choice of title. Bell—as a male relative of Woolf's, indifferent to his subject's feminist concerns, and playing the role of "authorised" biographer—emphasises Woolf's patriarchal surnames: the title of the first part of his biography is Virginia Stephen, that of the second Mrs. Woolf. Rose's feminist point of view is reflected in her title: *Woman of Letters: A Life of Virginia Woolf*. Finally, Gordon conveys through the title of her work a literary and intellectual slant: *Virginia Woolf: A Writer's Life*. Rose and Gordon devote far more attention to Woolf's works—both fiction and nonfiction—than does Bell; they could have found a rationale for their methodology in Woolf herself who, unlike some male modernists, believed in the connection between writers' experience and their work: ' "Every secret of a writer's soul, every experience of his life, every quality of his mind is written large in his works' " (Quoted by Gordon, 1984/1986, p. 6).

The ways Bell, Rose, and Gordon deal with Virginia Woolf's most autobiographical work of fiction illuminate some of the issues involved in the relationship between a biographer and his or her subject. Bell gives us the facts about the production of *To the Lighthouse:* the number of copies sold in the first year (3,873) and the curious detail that two of them were bought by the Seafarers' Educational Society (Bell, 1973, p. 129). Rose, on the other hand, is openly engaged in creating a feminist countermyth centered on the mother–daughter bond. After highlighting Mr. Ramsy as the archetypal domestic tyrant constantly demanding sympathy from his wife and Lily Briscoe, Rose reads *To the Lighthouse* as "Woolf's exorcism of her personal ghosts" and the classical account of "the tensions and fears that can afflict a creative woman" (p. 172). Gordon sees a more balanced portrait of Leslie Stephen/Mr. Ramsay in the novel. She examines Virginia's closeness to her father before his deterioration after the death of Julia Stephen, and eloquently describes the beauty of Woolf's presentation of Mrs. Ramsay, while commenting on the fact that, in *To the Lighthouse,* Woolf was writing "fictional biography, not biography proper" (p. 29). Gordon's account of the changing relationship between Woolf and her parents and the creation of Mr. and Mrs. Ramsay in the novel is an acute analysis of the possiblities and limitations of fiction as biography.

ENDINGS

I hope I have been able to trace some of the connections that exist between women's biography and women's fiction. I would like to dwell briefly on the always fascinating question of narrative endings. Both Victoria Glendinning and Fay Weldon finish their accounts of Rebecca West's life on an upbeat note. Having followed her subject's long life from beginning to end, Glendinning (1987) focuses on West's enduring achievement: "Her books remain and are read. That is what matters" (p. 249). Weldon (1985), leaving

Rebecca in 1914 after her baby has been born and she has been visited by Wells, looks forward to the future: "Start on the long road back to self-determination, to London, life without Wells, freedom and the future. It will take years, but you'll do it" (p. 104).

The ending of the more detailed, more intimate biography of Vita strikes an elegiac note. In many ways Vita is a figure irremediably of the past; her garden and her tower at Sissinghurst place her, by their very beauty, beyond the reach of any contemporary visitor. But the sense of achievement is paramount in these three biographies written by women. It is also interesting to compare them with biographies of Woolf. The celebratory note becomes difficult when the subject of the biography has committed suicide, but even so Bell (1973) gives us the bare details of Virginia's death: the fact that she put a large stone into her pocket and so on (p. 226), whereas Rose (1978/1986), while acknowledging the madness and the final despair, stresses the ordinariness of Virginia's fears and insecurities and the uniqueness of her art (pp. 262–266).

As a matter of fact, a contrastive reading of biographies of Woolf foregrounds some of the issues discussed elsewhere in this volume. Showalter (1977/1982) points out how most biographical accounts of Virginia Woolf's psychic disturbances concentrate on her troubled relationship with her father and overlook the connection with crises in female identity: "the first occurred in 1895, after the death of her mother and the onset of menstruation; the second from 1913 to 1915, after Leonard decided that they should not have children. Her suicide in 1941 followed menopause" (p. 267). When we turn to Quentin Bell's biography of Woolf, it is astonishing how many of the issues in Woolf's life and work which are crucial from a feminist viewpoint get short shrift in his account. Thus, for example, Bell (1973) uses a revealing simile in order to dismiss Woolf's pacifism: "Virginia hated violence—she associated it with masculine assertiveness. But were we then to scuttle *like frightened spinsters* [italics added] before the Fascist thugs?" (p. 186).

Bell (1973) also dismisses *Three Guineas,* arguably Woolf's most radically feminist work, on the grounds that the connection Woolf establishes between women's oppression and the threat of war is "tenuous" (p. 205). Rose (1978/1986) on the other hand sees *Three Guineas* as a highly relevant, still valid exploration of patriarchal mentality and of the ways "the very desire to make war derives largely from notions of manliness and from the desire to prove oneself a man, for which the old formulations of relationships between the sexes are responsible" (p. 218). Contemporary history bears Woolf out, since every single authoritarian regime—be it fascist or communist, right-wing Catholic or Islamic fundamentalist—has used the state ideological, economic, and educational apparatuses to suppress women's rights and to control their reproductive function.

It is not perhaps too surprising that women's biography raises some of the issues involved in approaching women's fiction from a feminist perspective: the existence of a muted women's culture, the problems of literary representation through a man-dominated language, the role of male critics/biographers, and so on. Women's biography, when written from a woman-centered point of view, can offer us what women's fiction does: access to suppressed female experience, imaginative empathy, a sense of achievement, and goals for the future.

REFERENCES

Bell, Quentin. (1973). *Virginia Woolf: A Biography* (Vol. 2). London: Hogarth Press.

Egerton, George. (1894). Virgin soil. In Christine Park & Caroline Heaton (Eds.), *Close company (stories of mothers and daughters)*. London: Virago.

Gilbert, Sandra M., & Gubar, Susan. (1988). *No man's land: The place of the woman writer in the twentieth century*. London: Yale University Press.

Glendinning, Victoria. (1983). Introduction. In Vita Sackville West, *The Edwardians*. London: Virago.

Glendinning, Victoria. (1983/1984). *Vita: The life of Vita Sackville-West*. Harmondsworth: Penguin.

Glendinning, Victoria. (1987). *Rebecca West*. London: Weidenfeld & Nicolson.

Gordon, Lyndall. (1984/1986). *Virginia Woolf: A writer's life*. Oxford: Oxford University Press.

Marcus, Jane (Ed.). (1982). *The young Rebecca: Writings of Rebecca West, 1911–1917*. London: Virago.

Rose, Phyllis. (1978/1986). *Woman of letters: A life of Virginia Woolf*. London: Pandora.

Sackville-West, Vita. (1923). *The challenge*. New York: Doran.

Sackville-West, Vita. (1930). *The Edwardians*. London: Hogarth Press.

Sackville-West, Vita. (1931/1983). *All passion spent*. London: Virago.

Schreiner, Olive. (1926/1982). *From man to man*. London: Virago.

Showalter, Elaine. (1977/1982). *A literature of their own* (British Women Novelists from Brontë to Lessing). London: Virago.

Tylee, Claire. (1988). *English literature and the construction of British memory of the First World War*. Unpublished PhD dissertation, University of Màlaga.

Weldon, Fay. (1971). *Down among the women*. London: Heinemann.

Weldon, Fay. (1975). *Female friends*. London: Heinemann.

Weldon, Fay. (1979). *Puffball*. London: Hodder & Stoughton.

Weldon, Fay. (1985). *Rebecca West*. Harmondsworth: Penguin.

Wells, H. G. (1909/1980). *Ann Veronica*. London: Virago.

Wells, H. G. (1911/1966). *The new Machiavelli*. Harmondsworth: Penguin.

West, Rebecca. (1918/1987). *The return of the soldier*. London: Virago.

West, Rebecca. (1928). *The strange necessity*. London: Jonathan Cape.

West, Rebecca. (1929). *Harriet Hume*. London: Hutchinson.

West, Rebecca. (1957/1984). *The fountain overflows*. London: Virago.

Woolf, Virginia. (1925). *Mrs. Dalloway*. London: Hogarth Press.

Woolf, Virginia. (1927). *To the lighthouse*. New York: Harcourt, Brace.

Woolf, Virginia. (1928). *A room of one's own*. London: Hogarth Press.

Woolf, Virginia. (1928). *Orlando: A biography*. London: Hogarth Press.

Woolf, Virginia. (1938). *Three guineas*. London: Hogarth Press. Reprinted 1977.

Woolf, Virginia. (1941). *Between the acts*. London: Hogarth Press.

Chapter 5

What Is a Feminist Biography?

Rachel Gutiérrez

Biography—a literary genre that arouses deep interest among so many readers, especially the English—began in Western culture to satisfy the curiosity about an individual who stood out among his contemporaries, and to try and understand him, to determine what made him exceptional. This traditional genre, the pattern of which is Plutarch's *Lives,* usually offers relevant clues to measure the creative genius of a poet, the original thoughts of a philosopher, the power of a political leader, the gift of an artist, or the achievements of a scientist.

Throughout the centuries biography has become one of the most popular genres although it has not been fully studied in its form and significance. Furthermore, there is no life of any woman among Plutarch's *Lives*. Western history has always been written by men and about men. The interest in women's lives has been limited to those who held men's positions—queens, empresses, women artists—or women who exerted power through men, wielding power as men and modeling their behavior on men. Adrienne Rich (1986) wrote that:

> As women our relationship to the past has been problematical. We have been every culture's core obsession (and repression); we have always constituted at least one-half, and are now a majority, of the species; yet in the written records we can barely find ourselves. (p. 86)

If nowadays more and more biographies of women have been written, it is because women today feel that their history has to be recorded to fill that gap and to bring to light, to uncover, and to recover the life of their forerunners—their peculiarities and the road taken by women to overcome the barriers in a world that, for centuries, has been ruled by men. Biography as a genre is important for feminism at a moment when the feminist theory is advancing more and more through the study of the work of social scientists, historians, and biographers who have undertaken research, gathering data and records.

About the specific work of the biographer, Alan Shelston (1977) explained:

> The biographer will overlap with the historian on the one hand, and with the novelist on the other, and while his source-material must inevitably be factual, the biographer has to deploy the techniques of the novelist, and here indeed lies his greatest difficulty. (pp. 65, 73)

It is worth noting the "historian" to date deals in the collective history of men's lives as has the biographer dealt in individual men. But aside from this, Victoria Glendinning (1988) states—after having published four successful biographies of women—that biography is "fiction under oath." If that is so, the biography of a woman should be written under a double oath: to the data and to the condition of women in history. It was feminism that brought to light the understanding of what being a woman means within the rigid limits of the patriarchal system, the ideology of which has maintained the double sexual standard and has prevented women from leading their lives independently—to develop their artistic gifts, to express themselves as professionals and as creative human beings. Accordingly, the woman who stands out is the one who, whether in her role in history, whether determined to challenge conventions, whether feminist or not, somehow becomes an example of independence and creative work: Therefore, her life should be made known.

The history of women is the history of their specific oppression, of the opposition the system has raised to their fulfilment and the power of resistance they have developed. Woman's "I" has always been handicapped. When a woman overcomes the limits imposed on her, and transcends the so-called "femininity," her struggle and her conquests assume a larger dimension and become a symbolic landmark in the social transformation of all women. Such social transformation of all women was implicit in the criticism voiced by some of them, extremely courageous, who proved with their lives that women's fate was not to become what the ideological rulers had cut out for them.

How was it possible for women who reflected their husbands's images—mirror-companions as they were, diplomatically obliged to bear out men's superiority by accepting their own inferior role—not to play that role to the point of total mutilation, even annulment, and succeed in doing something on their own, stubbornly believing in their own talent despite all forms of behavior to make them found to be wanting, or else, be called wicked because they shunned their role of help-mates, necessary and indispensable to the *other,* the Master. How much suffering, struggle, perseverance, and obduracy was required of them so that they would not give up and could arrive at expressing themselves and being heard. The interest in women's lives will fill in the huge vacuum left in historiography, introducing new significant protagonists in history.

Among these would be the Brazilian musician and composer, Chiquinha Gonzaga. Edinha Diniz (1984), who wrote her biography, explained:

> Her pioneering claim for personal freedom made her the first Brazilian figure in the History of Brazil, not a heroine in the official sense, she was neither at the service of her country, nor at the service of mankind, or at the service of a husband. She was only at her own service, according to her wishes and desires. Except that a woman was not permitted to do that. (p. 3)

Chiquinha Gonzaga is important in the development of the Brazilian culture. At the beginning of this century, when the majority of the Brazilian artists patterned their work on foreign values and models, she composed music from genuine Brazilian roots. Music scholar Andrade Muricy (quoted in Diniz, 1984) wrote that "no one before her marked so vigorously the Brazilian national spirit in our popular music." The biographer ascribes that phenomenon to the fact that:

> the woman at that time was usually a salon performer, still within the family circle and therefore in close contact with house slaves. Undoubtedly, that may have made the cultural interchange easier and resulted in a musical synthesis.

Chiquinha Gonzaga's work includes not only African rhythms but also succeeds in expressing the regional differences of a country as vast as Brazil. Critics said that her music could be "a poem of the Northeast," a "Rio de Janeiro landscape," or a "drama of the pampas." She could also write music in the style of Portugal. Her versatile talent led her to express herself in every form—from fashionable polkas and waltzes to the Brazilian "maxixe," from Carnival marches to salon tunes and operettas—and never lose the Brazilian characteristics. Her compositions amount to almost 2,000 pieces. Also extraordinary was Chiquinha Gonzaga's professional esprit do corps. She organized the first trade union to defend the copyrights of Brazilian musicians and playwrights. Using her prestige as an acclaimed conductor and composer, in 1917 she led the campaign to found the Brazilian Society of Playwrights. Her biographer further showed that "by refusing to play the conventional role of a wife and mother, she ended up by playing the role of a social reformer" (Diniz, 1984, p. 3).

The ideology of differentiated education tried to convince women that they were not entitled to voice any opinion, to arrive at any decision, or to have a profession or an artistic career. Her space was within the walls of the home, the street was man's domain. So much more extraordinary was, therefore, Chiquinha Gonzaga's career, at a time when "society established strict limits for the feminine space: the home for the woman, the *salon* for the lady, and the street for the slaves and the prostitutes" (Diniz, 1984, p. 4). She played her musical pieces at public houses!

Her biography emphasized how much a man can, rather than encourage a woman in her career, inhibit and thwart her aspirations, whereas women have always collaborated with men and goaded them to paths of glory. Women have acted as spring-boards in men's lives; men have placed hurdles in women's. So as to draw Chiquinha Gonzaga away from her piano, where she practiced for long hours, her husband would take her on frequent voyages, since he owned a merchant ship. It was the year 1865, during the war with Paraguay, exactly when the suffragettes were starting their struggle for the vote in England. Chiquinha Gonzaga's husband found himself between two wars: with Paraguay and with his wife, whose passion for the music and her need to express herself as a musician he wanted to thwart. Deprived of her piano she replaced it with a guitar that she somehow discovered onboard ship, and when he insisted that she choose between her music and her husband her answer was the characteristic: "Sir, I cannot conceive life without music" (Diniz, 1984, p. 67). She had borne two children, and when she once got back to Rio she discovered she was pregnant again. After her third child was born she left her husband and thus withstood the condemnation of both families—her own and her husband's—and went in quest of her artistic destiny.

Among musicians another example is Clara Schumann, herself a gifted composer, who devoted much of her life to playing her husband's music. When she had eight children and earned money as a pianist, how much time could she spare to write music? The time available to a woman for creative pursuits is usually curtailed, for she has her domestic obligations to attend to. A man can count on the support of the womenfolk at home: a mother, a wife, sisters, aunts, daughters. Alma Mahler, who was also gifted, was forbidden to have her musical compositions printed or to continue to compose. "From now on you have only one profession—to make me happy!" said Gustav Mahler when they were engaged, in a letter dated December 1901 (Françoise Zenakis, 1987, p. 164). One wonders if, had she married, could Emily Dickinson have ever written the poetry that is her important legacy to the American culture.

Some women have had to choose between motherhood and political participation, as Rosa Luxemburg did. Others have paid a high price for motherhood out of wedlock, as Rebecca West did. Simone de Beauvoir, engaged in public life and literature, chose to interrupt a pregnancy, and the same choice has been attributed to Lou Andreas-Salomé. Lou Andreas-Salomé has been mainly known as a woman who lived in a circle of outstanding men—Nietzsche, Rilke, Freud—as their disciple. Yet we know for certain that her ideas proved to be the seed that fertilized their work. One of her admirers says: "Once Lou falls in love with a man, nine months later he gives birth to a book" (H. F. Peters, 1986, p. 14). Her original ideas have been lately identified both in *Also spake Zarathustra* and in Rilke's poems, and Freud, many times, in the course of a 20-year correspondence with her, said that she was the poet of psychoanalysis. Her biographer (Peters, 1986) defined her as a woman brimming with ideas, daring in her speculations, and totally devoid of any hypocrisy, pretensions, and prejudices. If we consider the social taboos of her time, such virtues, rare among men, were not often found among women.

The Brazilian feminist Carmen da Silva, who started her magazine column 30 years ago, encapsulated in the story of her life a vivid picture of the women of her generation in the various countries of Latin America where she lived, and the background of the Brazilian society; its conventions are given a larger space in her narrative from the 1930s to the 1980s (Carmen Da Silva, 1984). About the title of her book, *Histórias Hibridas de Uma Senhora de Respeito* (Da Silva, 1984), she explained:

> "Histórias" (histories) because I refuse the Anglicism "estórias" (stories), with its mischievous intention of drawing a dividing line between the personal and the collective, cutting the links of individual successes in the course of History. The spelling with an "h" emphasizes my conviction that the private is political. "Hybrid" because they bring together my experiences and those of others, narrative and reflection, memories and gossip. Finally, "a Respectable Lady", despite its regrettable connotations that recall sanctimonious women, and women who march in the streets for family, church and property, because I did not find any other label more or less honourable for myself: a woman at an age bracket who, if not respectable, does not exist.

Carmen da Silva spoke of the "plural condition" of women, meaning the awakening of the collective spirit—that which the Anglo-Saxon may call "sorority"—after the historical self-awareness of the women in this century. That is why, when writing her biography, the writer tries to impart to us to what extent an individual life finds echo in other lives and, when doing that, showed us the political spirit of that discovery. Besides, at no moment in her book did Carmen da Silva restrain her sense of humor, her joy of living, her pride to be a woman.

Carmen da Silva is not just a great Brazilian writer. She is an example to all the militant feminists because, in her own words, she had had "a long and passionate love affair with liberty." Not all women have had such a wide participation in public life; it is up to the perceptive biographer to assess the limitations that women were confronted with to give their life real significance. Not all the women who went against conventions and succeeded, found themselves in a propicious stage of social change, as Claire Tomalin (1988) wrote about Katherine Mansfield's moment: "The moment seemed made for her and she for the moment" (p. 48).

Only in 1982, when Ann Delbée published the life of Camille Claudel, could the world learn of her tragic life and discover her original work as a sculptress. She was an equal to August Rodin, whose talented pupil and, later, mistress she was, as well as a disturbing competitor. Considered a revolutionary artist during the Belle Époche, she could beat the breathing bronze into the softest lines and capture the fleeting movement, drawing forth from marble the features of life, in an almost expressionist manner, where Rodin's had been mostly realistic. But her fame was shadowed by her master's and she had to pay for 30 years of creative work with 30 more years of isolation and abandonment in an insane asylum. What can be said of so many more women who remain unknown because neither sufficient information nor records are available to tell their lives?

That is why the biographer of women should be fully conversant with the patriarchal ideology to be able to assess precisely how much defiance their achievement expressed, and thus understand how important to the women of today is the road paved by the women of the past. When the biographer of a woman is a man he has to realize that—unlike the essayist who writes about what he knows, and closer to the fiction writer, who may often find himself helpless in the grip of his characters—he is going to sail into unchartered waters. He has not gone through the oppression and discrimination that women have experienced, thus his insight has to result from a deep study of and full commitment to his subject. A man should, however, have the sense of reality as Balzac had of the society he portrayed in his novels: Although he was under the spell of the aristocracy, he described the capitalist society with his keen power of observation and in its true colors. Marx and Engels considered Balzac's books the most perfect and reliable source of information about the characteristics of that society. If a man has that sense of reality he will bring out the portrait of a woman with the full background of women's reality.

So the man bent on writing a biography of a woman would have to divest himself of the privileges enjoyed by men in a world under male order. He would have to have free access to women's privacy, where children are under mothers' care, where domestic chores are performed. He would have to tell *her* story from the silent records of history, that inexhaustible fountain that for centuries only she nourished. Consequently, it could be said that a woman is more qualified to write about another woman. After biography discarded the 19th century prejudices which had caused Elizabeth Gaskell (1857) to omit Charlotte Brontë's sexual life, and after André Maurois's (1952) biography of George Sand included the details of her love life, women are now better qualified to enter the intimate world of the other woman who chose to challenge the prevailing Puritanism and not to thwart the force of their own sexuality.

Feminine space and women's history have been illuminated by feminism, a reality that can no longer be ignored. It is a theory that, starting from a critical view of society, asserts the historical meaning of women's struggle toward becoming fully developed individuals. Feminism is interested not only in exceptional women who grew to become as important as men, but also in those who were sacrificed by ideology, better defined as case studies, which are the subject of anthropology and sociology. Biography is about uniqueness. Nevertheless, the biography of the average woman, who has not distinguished herself from the majority, becomes the major subject of the political concern of feminist theory.

Feminism is today an avant-garde movement; it represents change in the interpretation of the world, as important as Marxism and psychoanalysis, for just as it is no longer possible to understand the unconscious mechanisms of human behavior without the contribution of psychoanalysis, nor the relation of production without taking into consideration the Marxist contribution, it is no longer possible to understand the relations between the sexes and the history of women without the contribution of the feminist outlook. Both in praxis and in theory feminism now stands at the point of no return. To write the history of women without the feminist point of view would be as unthinkable as to write history ignoring history. If the world were not what it is, that is, male-dominated, there would be no need for the feminist struggle, nor historical reason for feminism. Nor would culture have been enriched by the feminist Weltanschauung. Thus the framework of the biography of a woman written either by a male or female writer cannot overlook the feminist Weltanschauung: the vision and revision of woman's condition in history. This analysis is so significant that it encompasses a new interpretation of society as a whole. The contemporary outlook transforms past history into something different from the way it has always been regarded and, at the same time, helps to transform the present to foresee the changes in the future.

What better approach to understanding social injustice inflicted on women throughout the ages, than the biography of an exceptional woman for to speak of a woman as exception because she did not fit into the stereotype is already to denounce the injustice of stereotypes. By rebelling against the stereotype an exceptional woman stands out and is contrasted with those who submit to their stereotype. She also enables the other women to develop their virtual potentialities against all odds. In feminist political terms, that woman is more than just one woman, she is a mirror, a proposition, she is an existential project. It was because of such women who "invented" their lives, that in 1984, in her campaign for Vice-President of the United States, Geraldine Ferraro said that there are no longer doors that women cannot open. Roger Garaudy (1982) wrote that for some women, especially for those of the working class, to "become someone" implies becoming aware of the class oppression which brings men and women onto the same footing, but for the lower middle class and bourgeois, he makes a different emphasis: Achieving personal identity means confronting a domineering husband and companion. Garaudy seems to have forgotten that Engels qualified the working class women as the proletarians of the proletarian.

Because education is more accessible to women of the upper and middle classes it is possible that, for some time to come, still more biographies of privileged women will be written. This does not mean that the feminist movement does not benefit *all* women, whatever their class, because by criticizing the oppression of women and men, feminism is also criticizing the class system under which women are not only dominated by also exploited. Another privilege of the life of a middle or upper class woman is her relationship to money, a privilege that is not available to the majority of women.

From what I have written it is clear that the biography of any woman is part of history, history seen from the feminist perspective. The biographer should be totally involved not only with his or her character but also with woman's real world. In a last analysis I would say that the biography of a woman, if written honestly and well-founded, is bound to be a feminist biography.

REFERENCES

Da Silva, Carmen (1984). *Historias hibridas de uma senhora de respeito* [Hybrid histories of a respectable lady]. San Paulo: Brasiliense.

Delbee, Anne. (1988). *Une femme* [A woman]. (Martius Fontes, Ed.). Sao Paulo: Presses de la Renaissance.

Diniz, Edinha. (1984). *Chiquinha Gonzaga: Uma hitoria de vida* [Chiquinha Gonzaga: History of a life]. Rio de Janeiro: Codecri.

Garaudy Roger. (1982). *Liberacao da mulher, liberacao humana* [Woman liberation, human liberation]. Rio de Janeiro: Zahar.

Gaskell, Elizabeth. (1902). *Charlotte Brontë*. London: Haworth.

Glendinning, Victoria. (1988, July 21). Public Lecture. Women's Studies Summer Institute, University of London, London, England.

Maurois, Andre. (1952). *Lelia. Ou la vie de George Sand* [Lelia. Or the life of George Sand]. Paris: Hatchette.

Peters, H. F. (1986). *Lou: Minha irma, minha esposa* [My sister, my spouse—A biography of Lou Andreas-Salome]. Rio de Janeiro: Xahar.

Plutarch. (19??). *The lives of the noble Grecians and Romans*. (J. Dryden, Trans.). New York: Modern Library.

Rich, Adrienne. (1986). *Of woman born*. New York: W W Norton.

Shelston, Alan. (1977). *Biography*. London: Methuen.

Tomalin, Claire. (1988). *A secret life—A biography of Katherine Mansfield*. London: Penguin Books.

Zenakis, Francoise. (1987). *Zut! On a encore oublié Madam Freud* [Oh! Once again Mrs. Freud has been forgotten]. Rio de Janeiro: Rocco.

Part 2

Choices

In view of the issues discussed in the previous section, how can the biographer make clear to her reader what has been taking place between herself and her subject? How can she show the understandings behind the choices she has made: understandings that inevitably design and color the story she tells.

These three writers may have made the choices that you, the reader, would have made, but equally they may not have. They have chosen their subjects from their own personal enthusiasm and interest, and write original biographies inviting their readers to engage with the reasoning and feelings implicit in their choices. Consciousness of choice itself is highlighted as a continuous and fascinating part of the process rather than as a headache a writer must cope with at intervals in her work, a headache that is dissipated by recourse to consultation with experts and grand theory.

Meryn Stuart discusses how, in writing her biography of Marguerite Carr-Harris, she had to consider the influence that every biographer must have in creating her subject as a "character." Miriam Kalman Harris draws this theme further in her exploration of the work and life of Claire Myers Owens, of her responsibility in bringing to feminist attention a "lost" writer from recent history. Judith Jordan shows how and why she would wish to differ from another biographer in her version of the life of Isabella Bird.

Chapter 6

Making the Choices: Writing About Marguerite Carr-Harris

Meryn Stuart

Biography, the study of one person's unique life, is currently one of the most popular (and least studied) genres among women readers and writers—at least in the Anglo-American world. Women read biographies of other women because they want to know about their private worlds, about how other women perceived themselves and their lives, about their sources of power, as well as about how they incorporated work into their domestic lives. Women want to know these things because other women's experiences can be a resource to them, and because previously this resource has been denied (Dale Spender, 1988).

"Without a history," Alice Kessler-Harris (1988) tells us, "public policy follows the path of social myth," conflating all women into one monolithic whole. "Attention to historical reality encourages public policy makers to consider context, particularity and diversity" (p.237). Where biography assists feminist (and nursing) scholarship is in the very *individualizing* it permits. Many things only make sense as exemplified in the life of one person. Biographies provide us with the vivid, adventurous lives of women who coped in a particular society, at a particular time, and made choices in the face of that society's assumptions about proper female behavior. As historian Susan Trofimenkoff (1985) points out: "Biography can even be the laboratory for testing certain generalizations about a given society, a given so-

---

The writing of this biography is supported by a grant from the Hannah Institute for The History of Medicine.

cial movement, the process of social change, or even female behaviour itself" (p.4). In this paper, I wish to address these issues, as well as attempt to make explicit some of the complex methodological and theoretical issues involved in creating a feminist biography.

Marguerite Carr-Harris, who was born in 1879, was a spirited, fun-loving, articulate nurse whom I first discovered while writing a history of early public health nursing in Ontario (Meryn Stuart, 1987). In 1920, she was 1 of 16 nurses sent out by the central Provincial Board of Health to all parts of rural and northern Ontario, spreading the "gospel" of public health in an attempt to decrease childhood morbidity and mortality. The nurses were charged with the responsibility of demonstrating the usefulness and efficacy of a public health nurse, thereby convincing the towns to hire their own.

In the Archives of Ontario, I found a voluminous amount of data about these nurses and their work (see R.G. 10, series 30; R.G.62, series F;) But, of all the nurses, the extent and detail of Carr-Harris' correspondence and field notes bowled me over. Her intense commitment to the mission of the new public health movement, coupled with the exquisite diplomacy and tact she employed in difficult practice situations sometimes took my breath away. When I read her letters expressing the "feast of the soul" she experienced in "driving through glorious hills with none but the wild animals to disturb you," I probably knew that I would write more about her life.

WHY WRITE ABOUT THIS NURSE?

At this point, although the idea of writing Carr-Harris' biography was far from my mind, I was totally in awe of her, both as a practicing public health nurse and an independent "new" woman of the 1920s. Trying to keep health records on every settler in a northern district the size of Sweden, as well as battling typhoid, poverty, discrimination and the weather, she represented excellence to me. Because I had been a public health nurse (although in a rural, southern Ontario district), I could identify closely with her compassion for her patients' dilemmas and her commitment to her work.

However, she was not a "famous" person, neither a Florence Nightingale, nor a Queen Victoria. Nor did she marry a prime minister, or a renowned writer. She was an unmarried, upper middle-class white woman who became a nurse in the early 20th century, entered military service and was decorated, worked in the provincial child welfare project for 7 years, obtained her baccalaureate degree at age 50, and then retired to commune with family and friends until her death at age 85. She probably eschewed feminism—at least as we define it today—and had relatively conservative ideas about reform and woman's roles within it. She had no children, and she died without leaving an autobiography or oral testimony. What could impell me to write her biography and to call it "a feminist biography?"

I came to see Carr-Harris' life story as a resource to primarily other nurses, but also to historians and the public at large. The history of nursing and nurses—almost exclusively female—has been invisible and ignored by historians and even feminists, overshadowed by the history of medicine and the stories of the "great doctors." I believe that our task in writing nursing history is not a matter for the way many political and medical men are portrayed; that is: "he developed, he achieved, and he declined." Rather, we must *explain,* instead of focusing only on accomplishments (Susan Trofimenkoff, 1985, p. 7). An explanation of Carr-Harris' life and work would allow us to see the choices she made in the face of the constraints and opportunities of her time.

FEMINIST BIOGRAPHY

As a writer, I was driven to know WHY, to keep pushing until I found the answers to what compelled Marguerite Carr-Harris to strive so hard for excellence in her work and to choose a career over marriage. There were so few precedents or patterns for her to follow, although there were other women of her generation choosing nontraditional paths. Many of these were single women who experienced severe internal conflict in their efforts to be recognized as legitimate (see, for example, Joan Givner, 1989; Sharon O'Brien, 1987.) I also needed to tell the reading public that nurses played a valuable role in health care; I wanted to portray them as agents of social change, as active players in the history of health care. In some sense, I needed to justify my own choice of a nursing career to my newer, more radical self. When I was asked to write a biography of a nurse as part of a series of "Canadian medical lives" (in which Carr-Harris is the token nurse), I was elated and eagerly accepted. The process has proven to be much more difficult than I ever thought possible.

In 1928, Virginia Woolf lamented the fact that nothing was known about the way women experienced their lives in Elizabethan times. What men wrote about women was fictionalized; as she put it: "imaginatively she is of the highest importance; practically, she is completely insignificant. She pervades poetry from cover to cover; she is all but absent from history" (p.45). And what was it that prevented women from being heard? : the material conditions of their lives and the belief that women were inferior beings who needed protection by men. Add to this, one final blow according to Woolf (1928):

> Women have served all these centuries as looking glasses possessing the magic and delicious power of reflecting the figure of man at twice its natural

> size . . . Take [this power] away and man may die, like the drug fiend deprived of his cocaine. (p. 35–36)

I was vividly reminded of this quote—and of women's insignificance—as I was attempting to rediscover the life of Carr-Harris, whom I never met, and who has been dead for 20 years. Her elderly stepbrother whom I interviewed, was more interested in discussing *his* military and professional career than his sisters'. Her life was significant to him to the extent that she had provided him with treats from home during their common experience in the First World War, and had kept house for him during the time he pursued a master's degree. He really knew surprisingly little about her whereabouts most of her life, ignorant of where she had gone to school—or even if she had. He focused on her several suitors (noting that he had a picture of himself with one of them!), explaining that she had never married because "she couldn't make up her mind." (Isn't that just like a woman?) Carr-Harris' *nephew,* whom she supported financially and emotionally in his early life, could not tell me much more about her than her brother; he could not refer me to anyone who knew her, and in fact, expressed surprise that a number of women whom he had never seen before (or since) appeared at her funeral and had been her lifelong friends.

By this time, it should be clearer what I mean by "feminist biography," specifically historical biography. It is definitely *not* a matter of "reflecting men at twice their natural size." Feminist biography allows us to see women as central *actors,* and from the perspective of their own lived experience. Women's history has therefore attempted to "so redefine the canons of traditional history that the events and processes central to women's experience assume historical centrality, and women are recognized as active agents of social change" (Carroll Smith-Rosenberg, 1980, 56)

Secondly, feminist biography allows us to see gender as a historical construct. For, perhaps the most revolutionary aspect of contemporary women's history was the refusal to accept gender-role divisions as natural. Gender was man-made, the product of cultural definitions, not of biological forces. No universal femaleness or maleness existed. Rather economic, geographic, and ideational factors came together within specific societies to determine what rights, powers, privileges, and personalites women and men would possess. Thus "the intricate relation between the construction of gender and the structure of power became our principle concern" (Smith-Rosenberg, 1985, 12).

METHODOLOGICAL QUESTIONS

What form do biographies generally take? Depending on the biographer's (and reader's) inclinations and disciplinary background, biography may be seen as history, as literature, as art form, or as fictionalized "junk." In the same way, the biography may explain, glorify or assassinate the character under question, depending on the *intention* of the author and whom she or he perceives to be the audience for it.

In any biography, no matter what the purpose, a character, a life, and a story are woven by the author. Such metaphysical issues as subjectivity, objectivity, truth, reality, accountability, and validity are as relevant to biography as to any kind of research. Therefore, these questions are important to consider when one is attempting to disentangle the complex process of writing biography: How far is the "character" in biography an accurate representation, and how far the author's creation? How has the character been modified by the author, and how far has the author been modified by involvement with the character? And CAN we ever know the whole story, the Truth? And is this what our central concern should be in feminist biography? Is so-called "scientific objectivity" ever possible? (See Mary Poovey, 1988; Joan Scott, 1988).

To illustrate my thesis that the author does indeed create the character to a large extent (by her interpretation of sources and by her intention) let us consider biographies of the same person, written by different authors. Two—even three—biographies of one person may be unrecognizable as being about the same person, depending upon the interpretations of the authors. For example Cecil Woodham-Smith's (1951) biography of Florence Nightingale (borrowed heavily from Edward Cook) presents Nightingale as a rather sympathetic—if eccentric and brilliant—human being who was oppressed by her mid-Victorian family, and driven to work tirelessly to reform the British Army and establish the profession of nursing.

Contrast this with F. B. Smith's work *Florence Nightingale: Reputation and Power* which, I believe, sets out to turn her into a monster. He characterizes her as a "disposer of persons and objects" (p. 12), who spurned her loving, supportive and tolerant family and was only interested in her own personal and political power and good reputation. Descriptions such as "titillating fabulist" (p. 17), "manipulator" (p. 191), and "inexorable and untiring huntress" (p. 101) pepper the book and reveal an intense dislike for his character, as well as a psychoanalytic theoretical framework. And yet, Smith asserts (on the book jacket) that his book is a "full and alert reading" of Nightingale's life and work. Both Woodham-Smith and Smith are respected writers who undoubtedly stand by their work, and yet very dissimilar pictures of the subject emerge.

On the other hand, biographers such as Victoria Glendinning may at times seem to have a "formula" by which their various characters all sound somewhat alike because of the treatment given. She has written biographies of three well known British female literary figures: Rebecca West (Victoria Glendinning, 1987), Vita Sackville-West (Glendinning, 1983/1984), and Edith Sitwell (Glendinning, 1981). In many ways, all these women—who were contemporaries—begin to sound similar after reading about them: they were gifted, thwarted women who had difficult early family relationships and unhappy marriages. They attempted to create under numerous adversities, such as illegitimate children, neurotic relatives and unrequited (or conflicted) love affairs. All were wealthy at some time in their lives; in fact, Glendinning focuses, in each book, on the comings and goings of the upper classes and on a psychological interpretation of their lives. And yet, she believes that the biographer is "an artist under oath," who tells the truth—and must also write a good story. (Glendinning, 1988)

What do these authors' own backgrounds, biases, and "hidden agendas" have to do with writing credible and realistic biography? Or to be more precise, *how* does the author understand what she understands, using what evidence? (Liz Stanley, 1987, p. 30). To begin to answer this question, we need to look at the inverse half of the issue: How do authors get modified by characters, and does it matter?

Not surprisingly, there is good evidence that this process occurs, and that it does matter, at least to the outcome of the biography. In a fascinating book entitled *Between Women* (Carol Ascher, Louise de Salvo, & Sara Ruddick, 1984), writers described their "literary" relationships with the women about whom they wrote. They reported that it is far from easy to represent the complicated lives of women in a just and generous way. They talk about feeling emotionally swamped and overwhelmed by their subjects, about identification, and even about a kind of psychological transference. As subjects' lives are revealed, authors begin to examine their own lives, to reflect on similar experiences and to be transformed by this in ways never thought possible. They also report "stages in their relationship" with the often, deceased character, as well as how returning to earlier work on a subject after a major change in the author's own life can radically alter the way they reexperience the biography.

In a public lecture, Victoria Glendinning (1988) talked about being shaken by the knowledge of the "disastrous" relationship that Rebecca West endured with her son. Because of problems Glendinning was experiencing in her own family, the discovery of destructive mother–son relations in her subject's life made her reconsider her own situation. Joyce Antler's (1987) biography of Lucy Sprague Mitchell (born a year earlier than Carr-Harris) reveals that the author came to see her subject's life as a "model . . . for I saw myself grappling with many of the same personal and professional struggles" (p. ix).

British sociologist and biographer Liz Stanley (1987) believes that the way to do justice to women's lives is to see biography as a kaleidoscope: "each time you look you see something rather different" (p. 19). She believes that to omit the biographer's own autobiography is to "distort" reality. Versions of "shading" of biography into autobiography are rendered available to the reader as "essential elements" (p. 21): by this she means "the shifts, changes, developments, downturns and upturns in the way the biographer understands the subject with which she is involved" (p. 21). As these are woven into the text (or footnotes), a more honest and realistic picture emerges. This approach rejects "the truth" as a catch-phrase, in favor of "it all depends on *how you look and precisely what you look at*" [p. 30, italics added]. Layers of understanding and complexity are accumulated, according to the interpretive consciousness of the writer. Contrary to the beliefs of some biographers, these layers are not stripped away in order to reveal the real X or Y.

AUTOBIOGRAPHY AND BIOGRAPHY

As I write about Marguerite Carr-Harris, I am attempting to isolate my own interpretations by asking such questions as, Why am I interested in this particular issue? Why does her life interest me at all? How am I a part of the historical process with which I am engaged? The public health nurses in my study were told that they were responsible for the success or failure of the demonstrations. When Carr-Harris failed to get a nurse appointed in the town of Kenora, I identified with her, wanting to blame the two officials for being narrow-minded, feeling acutely my own fear of failure and wanting to see her as a victimized player in the situation. What would other—as yet unidentified—evidence have told me about the process of social change in a pivotal period of gender relations, politics, and economics? Why do I want to "prove" she was the victim? What are some of the strategies to represent a nurse's life and work evenly, and yet tell a readable story?

First, I have accepted the fact that one cannot "get it right," that there is no true "reality" about a life, and that inevitably the author's own "autobiography" must be woven with the biography. For example, what about another concern: that I have not identified with Carr-Harris *enough,* that I dislike her sometimes for her social class bias that looks too much like snobbery in pictures I have of her? Isn't one supposed to like one's subject?

Although I have not felt anything like being "emotionally swamped" by my subject, writing about her life has caused me to reflect a great deal on my own attitudes toward social class issues and health care. The writing has brought these issues into much greater relief for me. I moved from seeing her initially as a superhuman nurse who accomplished a great deal, to an upper class woman who felt compelled to "Canadianize" her immigrant patients, and finally, to seeing her as a woman who was doing the best she could with the conditions she faced, given her privileged background. I am still grappling with the problem of how to integrate *my* accumulated understandings of her life into the story.

Second, how do I handle large gaps in the story, when I do not know what was happening in her life? Will I suggest what I imagine she was doing and thinking, considering that I have never met her and only talked to some of her relatives who remember her from a very "subjective" perspective? And how is this different from fiction?

This raises issues related to the kind of evidence I am using, as well as how I am interpreting that evidence. Through secondary sources, primarily biographies of other "accomplished" middle-class women born at the same time, I have explained her life choices in terms of both the internal dynamics of her early family experiences and the external societal pressures that must have existed for her. Like many of her contemporaries, Carr-Harris' mother was ill for most of her daughter's childhood, dying when Marguerite was 11 years old. Her father was dominant in her life, both because he was reputed to be a strong, humanitarian individual but also because he was an adventurous risk-taker. The evidence available for her early childhood exists in photographs, biographies of her father and mother, and more importantly, in a surviving diary which Marguerite kept in her 12th year.

Third, assuming that I wish to *explain* Carr-Harris' life and work (rather than to glorify or condemn her), I now realize that I am indeed using biography as a testing-ground for generalizations about the interlocking contexts of womanhood, social class, community politics, and the medical hierarchy in public health. My central concern in all my research has been to examine the way in which particular conformations of gender and class informed decisions about rural public health work and, further, what this revealed about the deployment of power in contemporary society.

I want to know, through Carr-Harris' work, more about how nurses both transformed external constraints on their autonomy and yet reinforced the dominance of male medical authority. The key to discovering this process lies in exposing the relationships, both familial and professional, that can be examined in her life. Relationships have been both a source of oppression and joy for woman; however, they are always of interest for feminist writers for these very reasons. It is clear that every time one looks at another relationship, one sees something to make one view the subject's life differently.

I have attempted to make explicit some of the issues involved in writing a feminist biography as I have experienced them. I am convinced that it is important to examine one's own internal processes as an author. I continue to struggle with how to leave a "trail" in my work so that my own interpretations and biases will be evident in the development of the character. As Liz Stanley (1987) points out, writing down biographic processes "make visible the existence of something which is usually invisible and effectively denied" (p. 31). Breaking down the power divisions that exist between writers and readers is one of the truly feminist acts that writers can perform.

ENDNOTES

Approximately thirty boxes of documents in R.G. 10, series 30 and R.G. 62, series F relate directly to the public health nursing project. Another twenty boxes in R.G. 62, series B, D and E relate indirectly.

REFERENCES

Antler, Joyce. (1987). *Lucy Sprague Mitchell. The making of a modern woman*. New Haven: Yale University Press.

Ascher, Carol, deSalvo, Louise, and Ruddick, Sara. (Eds.) (1984). *Between women. Biographers, novelists, critics, teachers and artists write about their work on women*. Boston: Beacon Press.

Givner, Joan. (1989). *Mazo de la Roche. The hidden life*. Toronto: Oxford.

Glendinning, Victoria. (1981). *Edith Sitwell: A unicorn among lions*. New York: Knopf.

Glendinning, Victoria. (1983/1984). *Vita: The life of Vita Sackville-West*. Harmondsworth: Penguin.

Glendinning, Victoria. (1987). *Rebecca West*. London: Weidenfeld & Nicholson.

Glendinning, Victoria. (1988, July 21). Public lecture. University of London, Women's Studies Summer Institute.

Kessler-Harris, Alice. (1988). The just price, the free market and the value of women. *Feminist Studies, 14*(2), 235–250.

O'Brien, Sharon. (1987). *Willa Cather. The emerging voice. New York: Fawcett Columbine.*

Poovey, Mary. (1988). Feminism and deconstruction. *Feminist Studies, 14,* 51–65.

Scott, Joan. (1988). Deconstructing equality-versus-difference: or, the uses of poststructuralist theory for feminism. *Feminist Studies, 14,* 33–50.

Smith, F. B. (1982). *Florence Nightingale Reputation and power*. London: Croom Helm.

Smith-Rosenberg, Carroll. (1980). Politics and culture in women's history. *Feminist Studies, 6*(1), 55–64.

Smith-Rosenberg, Carroll. (1985). *Disorderly conduct. Visions of gender in victorian america*. New York: Alfred A. Knopf.

Spender, Dale. (1988, July). Women's Biography: Fact or Fiction. University of London, Women's Studies Summer Institute.

Stanley, Liz. (1987). Biography as microscope or kaleidoscope? The case of 'power' in Hannah Cullwick's relationship with Arthur Munby. *Women's Studies International Forum, 10*(1), 19–32.

Stuart, Meryn. (1987). 'Let not the people perish for lack of knowledge': Public health nursing and the Ontario rural child welfare project, 1916–1930. Ph.D. dissertation. University of Pennsylvania.

Trofimenkoff, Susan Mann. (1985). Feminist biography. *Atlantis, 10*(2), 1–7.

Woodham-Smith, Cecil. (1951). *Florence Nightingale*. New York: McGraw-Hill.

Woolf, Virginia. (1929). *A Room of one's own*. New York: Harcourt Brace Jovanovich.

Chapter 7
The Pressure of the Choices

Miriam Kalman Harris

Be wise and rush in where fools fear to tread. Claire Myers Spotswood (Owens) The Unpredictable Adventure

"How do you know how to go about it?" asked an artist friend.

"I don't. I have to make it up as I go along."

"Oh," she responded. "Like painting a painting."

Yes, I thought. Like painting a painting, from scratch, when you don't know how to paint: Like recreating something you've seen in an entirely new form, without knowing exactly what you know about the subject or how you want it to look until the creation emerges before you. Like watching the paint flow onto a canvas and realizing yes—that is what it looks like.

But I am no painter. I am a writer painting a portrait in words of a deceased woman I have never met. I intend to bring her back to life as colorfully and as powerfully as the painting hanging on the wall of Elizabeth Snapp's office at Texas Women's University (TWU).

Interesting: The way I first discovered Claire Myers Owens was through that painting—a water color portrait of the woman herself. Or should I say lady? For Claire lived her entire life balancing herself between the two images, struggling to define herself as a woman while never entirely giving up the image of herself as a lady. But I am getting ahead of myself. First, the portrait. Then the woman, her life, and her work.

From the first time I read Charlotte Perkins Gilman's (1973) *The Yellow Wallpaper,* I knew that I wanted to participate in the contemporary feminist adventure of rediscovering and republishing "lost" women writers, gathering together their voices from the silent pages of literary and cultural history, filling the void with women's voices that echoed the perspective, experiences, insights and world views that had been missing from my generation's—indeed, all previous generations'—formal education.

It was with this simple (or so it seemed to me then) objective in mind that, some years later, I obtained an appointment with Elizabeth Snapp, Director of Libraries at TWU, in order to preview the available archives with the hope that I could rescue a heroine/writer whose life and work might be buried there. We sat in her office over coffee while Elizabeth Snapp reviewed the contents of the archive itself, catalogued from memory the achievements and contributions of women, living and dead, resting in their files. Hours passed as we shared common interests, feminist literary concerns, and favorite books and authors. And always, always: the portrait. That woman—beautiful, formidable, vulnerable, looking out from the wall, seeming (was I completely crazy?) to participate in our discourse, casting her enigmatic gaze of approval, demanding an audience to her own concerns.

Claire Myers Owens, Elizabeth Snapp volunteered as my eyes reached above her head for the millionth time, graduated from TWU (then the College of Industrial Arts) in 1916 with a Bachelor's Degree in Domestic Science. A native Texan, she lived most of her adult life in the Northeast—New York and Connecticut. She took up Zen Buddhism at age 70, studied transpersonal psychology, became a respected member of the human potential movement—lecturing, interviewing, and writing books and essays almost up to the time of her death.

Books? Did she say books? What kind of books?

Oh, three or four autobiographies, one novel—a fantasy with a female heroine modeled after James Branch Cabell's Jurgen series.

Could I see her work; could I read her books?

Claire's was a closed file; no one had been allowed to work in her archive since they were first processed. Even now, the boxes retain their label, "Closed." Ms. Snapp later confided that she had held Claire's file back hoping someone would come along she felt she could trust to relate to Claire and what she stood for. She was special, unique. Not everyone would appreciate her work; not everyone would understand. As she observed my interest in Claire's story, an inner voice told her "this is the one." She believes that inner voice was the voice of Claire herself. From what I have learned about Claire since I first came to know her, I do not doubt for a minute that it was. And why the mystery? Why the closed boxes? Elizabeth Snapp only smiles and winks, implying there are reasons.

Claire's is a story of self-discovery, an adventure that begins in 1896, in Rockdale, Texas—a small town in the heart of the "bible belt," a town she renames in her fiction "Smug Harbor"—and ends four published books, numerous essays, articles, unpublished manuscripts, three husbands, and

87 years later in Rochester, New York in a Zen Buddhist colony. Reared by fundamentalist Baptist parents who disinherited her when, after graduating college, she broke with traditional teachings and set out on her own path, Claire, nevertheless, lived most of her life as a member of the privileged class. Rarely were her struggles to survive economic. Rather, Claire's struggles were internal and intellectual: her drive to define herself as an autonomous woman against the expectations of a social milieu that defined her as a lady, a Southern Belle. Later, as an adult married to the economically successful and socially prominent banker, H. Thurston Owens, she fought to maintain a sense of individuality and autonomy against the conventions of a community that embraced her as a member of the New England social elite. During each phase of her life's journey, Claire encountered obstacles that sought to rob her of her hard won self-perceptions. During each phase, each encounter, Claire emerged in charge of her Self and her life.

Claire's portrait haunted my drive home that first evening. My fascination with the painting was as much a tribute to the skill of the artist as an intuitive response to the force of the woman behind the portrait. The name of the artist who painted the picture of Claire is Minna Walker Smith. There is no date on it, but it would have been painted in the 1940's after Claire married H. Thurston Owens and was living in New Haven, Connecticut. I felt an overwhelming need to see the portrait again sensing that somehow it would dispel my fears and answer my questions: Who was I to take this on? What did I know about transpersonal psychology, Zen? How would I be able to evaluate her work in these areas? Perhaps I should drop the whole thing before I became involved in something outside my field and continue to search for a writer of mainstream literature, someone I could count on to provide me with literature I could recommend with a feeling of certainty. But Claire was a woman—writing about being a woman. And even if she didn't define herself as a feminist, I sensed from what little I knew about her and from the aura that emerged from the portrait, she would not have rejected consideration as a feminist heroine. It would be inappropriate to call Claire a feminist. She did not align herself with the movement in the sixties and seventies. Nor was she particularly interested—as least as far as I can tell in her autobiographies, fiction and letters—in the suffrage issues of 1916, the year she graduated college and set out on her own, against the traditions of her family. Still, I do not believe it is inaccurate to identify Claire as an individualist whose life goals, even as early as age twelve, reflect the feminist motif of self-discovery and self-definition, whereby realization and fulfilment come from within.

In a sense, the author's name becomes something of a feminist issue. Her first book, the novel *The Unpredictable Adventure,* was published under the name Claire Myers Spotswood (Claire Myers Spotswood, 1935). Afraid to rely on her perception of herself as strong, independent, and knowledgeable, Claire borrowed the name Spotswood from an old family connection of aristocratic heritage in order to add authenticity and credibility to her image. Reviewers touted her as "Miss Spotswood, of the Virginia Spotswoods" to exploit her prestigious connections. As reported in the Hartford Times, May 18, 1935, "Miss Spotswood is a descendent of . . . Alexander Spotswood who was royal governor (of Virginia) under Queen Anne from 1710 to 1722." These roots connect Claire to Martha Washington, a descendent of the same Spotswoods. Shortly before publication of her novel Claire married journalist George Wanders. Her articles and reviews published during the course of this brief marriage bear the name Claire Myers Wanders; and at one point, after her divorce, she is referred to in print as Mrs. Claire Spotswood Wanders. Her name keeps changing. It is only in 1958 with the publication of her second book at age 62 that she becomes professionally identified as Claire Myers Owens, which she sticks with for the next 25 years. Therefore throughout this essay, I have chosen to refer to her as Claire: It is the one name that is consistently and unchangeably her own throughout her life.

From the first few hours I spent perusing the contents of her archive, I was hooked: hooked, confused, dismayed, elated. I sensed that Claire Myers Owens was indeed a rare find. I was impressed: evidence in her earliest writings—even in childhood—poses questions that anticipate the current right brain/left brain theories of creativity, theories she spent the latter years of her life investigating. Her novel and her later work with the transpersonal psychology movement anticipate our contemporary women's spirituality movement. Her intellectual curiosity remained vibrant all her life. But she was an enigma: a contradictory, paradoxical woman, part feminist, part Southern Belle, as flirtatious and coy as she was bold and controversial; as intellectually curious as she was stubborn and defiant, inconsistent in her professional pursuits, babbling one minute, profound the next. And frustrating! With the success of *The Unpredictable Adventure,* even in the face of an ensuing scandal, she was contracted by Burton Rascoe at Doubleday to write seven more novels for a series. A brief newspaper blurb mentions that she started a second, yet I found no evidence of it in her files or in her personal letters and no sequels were ever published. Although her bachelor's degree in domestic science was forced on her by her father—she wanted to study literature and philosophy at the University of Texas but he insisted that choice wasn't proper for a "lady"—she never stopped studying, learning. Her reverence for wisdom and knowledge inform every book, article, and essay she ever wrote. Yet she refused to enter any formal postgraduate degree program that would have allowed her to raise the level of her writing; she spent years attending Yale University as a special student of literature, philosophy, and psychology—reading, writing, and lecturing on her own terms, corresponding with some of the greatest (male) minds of the

20th century: Havelock Ellis, Aldous Huxley, Bertrand Russell, H. L. Menken, Joseph Campbell, Abraham Maslow, James Branch Cabell himself, and even Carl Jung. Yet the essay she wrote after her personal interview with Jung in Paris is rather light and anecdotal. Claire visited Jung on July 24, 1954 and wrote up the experience for a contest feature, "Tourists Abroad," in the Paris edition of the *New York Herald Tribune*. Her article was the winning entry for August 12, 1954 (Claire Myers Owens, 1954). In this light, perhaps my judgment of it is too harsh: For its purpose, it won acclaim. However, in view of Claire's deep admiration for Jung's work it is remarkable and disappointing that she never wrote anything substantive about that interview although she refers to it briefly in later writings (Owens, 1958, 1963). Nevertheless, her work at various times of her life brought praise from highly respected men in her field (there were surprisingly few women interested in her even during the 1970s and 1980s).

After several weeks of careful reading, I made the following observation in my notes concerning her four published books:

> Her writing as it spans a period of over forty years is uneven, with a tendency toward melodrama and clichés. I'm trying to get through it and see what I'd do about the level of writing and thinking I find in her first two autobiographies. However, her first novel and last autobiography exhibit a higher literary level and offer invaluable sources of insight into a feminist spirit and approach to living. (Owens, 1958, 1963, 1979; Spotswood, 1935)

Later notations indicate that while I was put off by Claire's voice, which I found "too didactic, personal" and finally "fragmented into a cacophony of voices which never became harmonious, symphonic," I had to admit that it was this same quality that gave her work value and substance. "I have quite frankly never read anything more honest, never found any books that reveal more recognizable fears, joys, pains and rewards."

Without knowing it, I had hit upon the essence of feminist theory and methodology—the personal connection Liz Stanley (1987) describes as the "living relationship" (p. 30) that evolves between the biographer and her subject, which, as I was experiencing it, fluctuated between admiration on the one hand and reservation on the other. But I could not have justified, from an intellectual perspective, the process as it was affecting me at that time. I had expected the research to be simpler. I expected to meet a woman in the archive, fall in love with her work, and with great joy and certainty, proceed to evaluate it.

In some ways, that is what happened. When I first started reading women's literature, years earlier, I know that part of the attraction was the way I found myself and my own perceptions reflected in the experiences and insights of the authors and their protagonists. My notes reveal I had that same feeling reading Claire:

> Like Claire Myers Owens says, you don't understand anything until you've already thought it and begun "to recognize the world from that angle." That

angle is female and Claire never lets up, never backs down. So what if I must wade through a few extra pages and a few repetitions? It is worth it for the insights, the honesty, the way she has of telling me what I always knew without knowing I knew it.

I clearly admired her life and character: her flexibility and courage, her strong belief in herself, her persistence and tenacity in pursuit of both worldly wisdom and self-knowledge. I noted that her autobiographical writings "provide profound self-insight and baffling observations on mysticism and spirituality, along with Jungian patterns reflecting the divided self and the process of individuation." Her novel, I wrote, "elicits profound observations on male–female love relationships," and "introduces themes of mythical quality and proportion that establish a 'mythology of love,' consisting of rites and ceremonies using female-conceived imagery and symbolism." Yet other notations clearly reflect my ambivalence and doubt: if some of her work was acceptable, some of it even wonderful, much of it was unscholarly, unpolished. I wanted more. I wanted consistency. I wanted perfection. Like Tellectina, the protagonist of Claire's novel, I wanted Certitude.

The Unpredicable Adventure is a fantasy in the Cabellian mode with Tellectina as a female Jurgen set on a voyage of self-discovery. Tellectina leaves her hometown of Smug Harbor in the Land of Err to travel in the Forbidden Country of Nithking, an anagram for thinking. The use of anagrams establishes an allegorical pattern: people and places become symbols of obstacles and insights, goals and psychological conditions. The heroine strives to reach the top of Mount Certitude where she will be able to look out upon the Truth, where she will know, and attain her ultimate goal of Self-Realization. Tellectina Femina Christian. Like the name game the author plays in real life, names represent aspects of the protagonist's psychological indentity. Tellectina, the intellectual, curious, aggressive, male-modeled self is pitted against Femina, antagonist to all worldly pursuit, the passive, lady-like, nurturing, seductive and yet male-identified self. These two "natural sisters" meet unexpectedly during Tina's first day of college and throughout the rest of the novel emerge and interact with one another as separate selves, each arguing, foiling, and tricking the other in an effort to win control. Each persona is a natural component of a psychically whole female; however, neither can develop into a natural wholeness because each has been split off from the other by the moralistic upbringing the surname represents. Christian becomes that aspect of the protagonist that functions as a cultural superego or patriarchal conscience, structuring the two personae, which appear, disappear, divide, and reunite as the adventure unfolds. that functions as a superego or patriarchal conscience, structuring the other two personae, which appear, disappear, divide, and reunite throughout the novel.

Aunt Sophistica Tellectina Christian—a fun-loving unmarried, independent woman who defies the world to call her spinster—serves as role model, mentor, spiritual guide, and namesake. As Tellectina sets off on her adventure into Nithking, Aunt Sophistica admonishes her *not* to be careful, but to "Be wise and rush in where fools fear to tread;" *not* to let her conscience be her guide, but "desire." "Abandon yourself recklessly to the passion of living . . . throw yourself into this expedition with a whole heart—half measures are for puny people. . . . Be the grand amoureuse of life" (p. 73–74).

Aunt Sophistica warns Tina of the hazards of the journey and humorously instructs her in ways that lay out the feminist tracts of the novel, satirizing patriarchal society and a host of Christian-endorsed institutions. As Sophistica reverses the platitudes a good Christian girl would have grown up obeying, so she reconstructs the Ten Commandments, humorously molding them into what might be considered a feminist bylaw (p. 75). Her diatribe against the sexual double standard could serve as a feminist framework for a treatise on morality and sexual freedom. Her discourse on the injustice of required virginity for unmarried women and society's derogatory labeling of "spinster" becomes a linguistic critique of patriarchal illogic when it comes to naming women's experiences and perceptions and defining their needs.

All this advice is delivered with a sense of humor and joy: life is a game, an adventure. Truth is not found on Mount Certitude but on Mount Ghaulot (meaning to laugh) "where the atmosphere is so clear one can see to the very ends of the earth" (p. 90). But laughter and humor, as Aunt Sophie tells us, are not born of joy but of suffering; our heroine must endure the painful lessons of life in order to learn to laugh both at herself and at the visions of reality she has been taught.

As her lessons reverse male truisms, patriarchal values, and fundamentalist religious teachings, they erase past understanding. Tina is left facing a "blank page," confronted by decisions that force her to realize her own truth—which was her goal in the first place. But the gap, the empty patches of the unknown leave her with an even greater need for Certitude. The most painful lesson Tellectina must learn—the lesson Claire had to learn to achieve self-definition, the lesson I had to learn in order to be able to write about Claire—is that there is no place called Certitude. There is no such thing as a "predictable" adventure. If it is predictable it is not an adventure.

The most exciting aspect of this remarkable book describes Tellectina's experiences in the Seven Siren Islands, where Femina's personality rises to its greatest strength (pp. 241–300). Here, the author invents a ceremony of female sexual initiation. The erotic symbology reverses our expectations and describes rites of passage designed by a woman to satisfy her own secret fantasies. Translated through allegory to a mythical level, these rituals become an exploration of female passion and an expression of woman's basic desires and sexual needs.

It is no wonder that the book received rave reviews all over the country when first released. Nor is it surprising that it was banned by the New York public library and removed from its shelves. As a reviewer claimed in the Richmond, Virginia *News Leader* on October 21, 1935, *The Unpredictable Adventure,* which sought "to tell the world about woman's search for happiness" showed prospects for financial success until it was banned by the new York public library because "it was too risque for its shelves. The author, who writes in the Cabellian mood, had said too much about the strange affairs of Tellectina in the Land of Nithking." The Los Angeles *Times,* October 27, 1935, hailed the novel in one sentence as reminiscent "of Pilgrim's Progress" with "double meanings, anagrams," and in the next disclaimed it as "an allegory of a woman's adventures . . . more instructive than most manuals about what a young girl ought to know." Miss Claire Myers Spotswood was scandalized; her reputation demolished!

Contemporary feminists have learned to be on the alert for "bad" women. Social convention labels "bad" any woman who stands outside the acceptable norm, any woman who wants to know more about herself and the world than is generally approved. The banning of Claire's book in 1935 was a signal to me to look carefully at its themes, language, and concerns. For, through this book not only do we learn more about what women need to know about themselves, we observe, once again, society's repression of what women need to know at all.

Arriving at this conclusion, from the first time I read it, I now found I was completely sold on the value of reprinting *The Unpredictable Adventure*. I knew the book would be a valuable asset to women's studies courses. In addition to its exciting literary qualities, the book offers provocative material for studies in women and psychology, spirituality, myth and ritual, and heroic patterns. Yet even as time passed, I found myself reluctant to compose a query and send it to feminist publishers. Why? What exactly were my reservations?

My concerns centered around Claire's inconsistent levels of writing as well as her values as a person: Is Claire a "proper" feminist heroine? What relevant criteria should I use to determine if her life deserved, or could stand up to, the close scrutiny required by biography? What relevant criteria should I use to justify reprinting her first and only novel? Her autobiographies? For every plus concerning her life and her work I could find a minus. I considered my reservations and decided the kinds of projects I had in mind were too important, too significant, and too complex to risk my taking a naive approach. I determined to seek the advice of the experts before I proceeded, a decision which led me to an "unpredictable adventure" of my own: a 4 week study with Dale Spender at the University of London's Women's Studies Summer Institute and my first trip to Europe. With a suitcase full of notes, a xerox copy of *The Unpredictable Adventure,* copies of reviews of Claire's books, and a scrambled assortment of scribbled questions and considerations—inconsistencies and doubts that time had not resolved—I headed for "Nithking" and "Mount Certitude."

Dale Spender responded positively when I first described the Claire Myers Owens archive. I felt my project was in good hands. Spender makes her experience in writing and publishing available to those of us who want to contribute to the growing store of feminist knowledge. Her confirmation that as contemporary feminists we are the authorities of our own insights, empowered me to empower myself.

The twists and turns of my private adventure—shared with like-minded women from a variety of countries—enlarged my understanding of the writing process as it clarified my perception of my role as biographer. The feminist biographers we studied and met confirmed my earlier beliefs and intuitions even as they introduced new ideas, new concepts. Liz Stanley, editor of *The Diaries of Hannah Cullwick* (1984) and author of numerous essays on the subject, and biographer Victoria Glendinning (1982, 1984, 1986, 1987) generously shared the benefits of their professional experiences and observations. The lives researched and celebrated in Dale Spender's (1982, 1983, 1986) many biographical sketches provided a wide range of insights. But the most important benefit of this focused study was the relaxed nurturing that accompanied the feminist mentoring process.

Dale Spender in various lectures has suggested that the first step is to allow myself the freedom of authority to choose my own heroines according to my perceptions, values, and understanding. As we uncover the writings of our foremothers, as we measure them against our own perceptions and experiences, we revalidate their writings and their lives. There is no other way to go about inventing and defining ourselves or our heroines (Spender, 1982, 1983, 1986).

Liz Stanley introduced the metaphor of a kaleidoscope to describe the phenomenon of change involved in the practice of writing biography: "each time you look you see something rather different; perhaps composed of the same elements but in a new configuration" (p. 19). We learn through evaluation of the material we discover, and we evaluate as we learn. It's an ongoing, unending, and circular process. Although certain phases of the process will come to closure when a book or article goes to press, knowledge and discovery function on a continuum, influencing the perspective of future projects. My relationship with Claire as I continue to read, interview, research, and expand my understanding of who she was, what she stood for, what we share as women and as human beings, how we are alike and how we are different, will expand into an even more complex relationship, a "kaleidoscopic" relationship, that outlives the parameters of the projects I eventually define. Accepting this, I also realize that just as I do not have the right to judge Claire, so I must abandon the idea that it is my role and responsibility to justify her weaknesses.

When Liz Stanley encourages us not to confine feminist biography to feminist heroines—"I'm not saying no heroines, just not entirely heroines" (1987, p. 22)—she reminds us that too often in our culture we operate under the misconception that to be heroic is to be strong, powerful, and flawless, and to be a feminist heroine is to be flawlessly feminist. Men have never had to be perfect in order to be considered significant and in order for their lives to be celebrated as heroic (e.g., Oedipus, Constantine, Ulysses, Ceasar). Why should women? That is to say the "what went wrong" in Claire's life and career is equally as important as the "what went right." If we are looking for models it is important to see and know about the opportunities seized as well as the opportunities missed. Claire did not see herself in terms of success or failure. She saw herself as a pilgrim, a pioneer, an adventurer. As we choose our heroines, as we tell their stories, as we hold their creative works up to contemporary study, we reveal *our* notion of the heroic. The only way to arrive at a feminist definition of the heroic is to allow the heroine to define herself—using our eyes, our voices, and our vocabulary to recreate her experiences. Our autobiographies merge with the heroines' biographies; the stories that emerge reveal the values and cultures of *both* characters.

During the months since I returned from London I have searched for the terms which would allow me to settle my confusion (for the time being) about this story of myself and Claire. Looking back to books I used in previous projects, I rediscovered an earlier work by Liz Stanley (1983), written in collaboration with Sue Wise, which explores the nature of the feminist research process in general. Here I found the seeds of Stanley's current theories on writing feminist biography and a vocabulary for articulating my experiences of doubt and confusion as well as my new resolutions.

Stanley and Wise (1983) explain that traditional research uses a "positivist model." The first stage involves the "formulation of hypotheses which express the nature of the problem or interest to be investigated." The second stage involves devising a "technical procedure" to gather appropriate data. The third stage involves an analyses of the data that then measures the data to see how it "fits" the formula. Feminist research, according to Stanley and Wise, is inductive and natural: The naturalist model describes a research process in which the "theory comes out of the research rather than preceding it." The researcher, thus, enters a natural setting—the archive—lives in it, and then produces a description of the setting and a "theoretical interpretation of what has occurred within it." Of course, for me and the relationship I have formed with Claire, this approach makes sense. (pp. 151–175).

When I first began to read about Claire my hypothesis, according to my notes, was as follows:

> What is missing from our literary canons is a sweeping and comprehensive new definition of the image, role, ideal, indeed the very word itself: Heroine. Biography, in a sense, works toward that new definition. Reprints of lost works reinforce the relevance and power of the lives we study. The real heroine is

> the one who succeeds and fails and then finds ways to succeed once more. On her own terms. No matter the values of the world she is situated in.

Lofty! And unfair. Indeed, the very concept of such a literary canon implies the existence of an impersonal judgment of that which deserves to be included. Such a notion goes against the very grain of feminist ideals defined herein. No wonder I felt lost, confused, and ambivalent. I was trying to fit a feminist project into a non- or even antifeminist framework. Not to say feminism does not need or endorse a canon of literature. Indeed, we are beginning to formulate canons through women's literature classes and through anthologies collecting writings by women. However, although one of my goals may be to add to such canons, I needed a dynamic, supple approach to allow me to identify a work worthy of feminist analysis and eventual celebration. Without realizing it, my expectations had been influenced by traditional methodologies that would have established a set of criteria and expected the work to fit in it.

Although Claire did not consider herself a feminist, I do not believe she would reject my identification of her as a heroine. Because of her lifelong struggle toward self-definition and autonomy, she makes an appropriate subject for a feminist study. But only on her own terms—as revealed through the story her life tells—and not according to a set of criteria she never knew existed but would be, if not in life then in death, expected to live up to.

From my search in London for Certitude, I returned with my original goal confirmed: to republish Claire's first published work, *The Unpredictable Adventure* and to write an introduction contextualizing the circumstances of the author's life and an afterword analyzing the significance of the book as an artistic accomplishment and feminist document. I returned with a more realistic, systematic approach to achieving my aims, along with a more manageable approach to addressing the questions. I returned also with the realization that many of my doubts about the value of Claire's life works were evidence of self-doubt about my own competency to deal with the problems inherent in my project. I have learned that the courage of conviction the writer must summon grows out of the self-affirmation that results when we make choices, not in anticipation of revealing one truth, but in anticipation of contributing to an enriched understanding of our subject, based on an expression of our own, personal truths. What is "right" for us today we must understand differently tomorrow. We must give ourselves permission to be "wise and rush in where fools fear to tread," and to work with the models we have, connecting our generation not only with generations in our distant past, but also with our more recent past to disallow the gaps in our histories and to stay vitally audible, continually visible.

Like painting a painting, I begin with a blank canvas, an empty page. I begin with a vision of Claire—who she was, how she thought, why she chose to live as she lived—but the vision is distant, cloudy, shimmering with mystery. I begin with that mystery. I begin with an idea of Claire and her life as a worthy subject, and the conviction that her first novel is an important resource for contemporary understanding of female identity as a process of self-discovery and self-perception. Her voice in my ear, my pen in my hand . . . I begin.

REFERENCES

A girl ought to know. (1935, October 27). *Los Angeles Times.*

Gilman, Charlotte Perkins. (1973). *The Yellow Wallpaper.* Old Westbury, NY: Feminist Press. (Original work published 1899)

Glendinning, Victoria. (1982). *Edith Sitwell: A unicorn among lions.* New York: Knopf.

Glendinning, Victoria. (1984). *Vita: The life of Vita Sackville-West.* England: Penguin Books.

Glendinning, Victoria. (1986). *Elizabeth Bowen.* New York: Avon.

Glendinning, Victoria. (1987). *Rebecca West: A life.* New York: Knopf.

Murray, Marian (1935, May 18). Her first book will be published in September. *Hartford Daily Times,* p. 9.

Owens, Claire Myers. (1954). Horns blowing, bells ringing. *New York Herald Tribune* (Paris). In William McGuire & R. F. C. Hull (Eds.) (1977), *C. G. Jung speaking* (pp. 237–239). Princeton, NJ: Princeton University Press.

Owens, Claire Myers. (1958). *Awakening to the good.* Boston: Christopher Publishing House. Republished as *Small Ecstasies* (1983). San Diego, CA: ACS Publications.

Owens, Claire Myers. (1963). *Discovery of the self.* Boston: Christopher Publishing House.

Owens, Claire Myers. (1979). *Zen and the lady.* NY: Baraka Books.

Spender, Dale. (1982). *Women of ideas—And what men have done to them.* London: Routledge & Kegan Paul.

Spender, Dale (Ed.). (1983). *Feminist theories: Three centuries of women's intellectual traditions.* London: The Women's Press.

Spender, Dale. (1986). *Mothers of the novel: 106 good women writers before Jane Austen.* London: Pandora Press.

Spotswood, Claire Myers (1935). *The unpredictable adventure.* New York: Doubleday, Doran & Company, Inc.

Stanley, Liz & Sue Wise. (1983). *Breaking out: Feminist consciousness and feminist research.* London: Routledge & Kegan Paul.

Stanley, Liz (1984). Introduction. In Liz Stanley (Ed.), *The diaries of Hannah Cullwick: Victorian maidservant.* London: Virago Press.

Stanley, Liz. (1987). Biography as microscope or kaleidoscope? The case of "power" in Hannah Cullwick's relationship with Arthur Munby. *Women's Studies International Forum, 10*(1), 19–31.

Williams, Murat. (1935, October 12). Unheralded Virginia novelist "thrilled" over reception of her first book. *Richmond News Leader,* About Books.

Chapter 8

Telling Choices in the Life of Isabella Bird

Judith Jordan

Isabella Bird was a Victorian traveller who journeyed alone to virtually inaccessible parts of the world, places then almost unknown to the English reading public. Journeys were then more arduous than they are now; people were truly out of touch for months at a time. Often Isabella Bird, as the first white woman the native population had seen, incited intense curiosity.

She incited my curiosity when, leafing through a lavish picture book, *Backroads of Colorado* (Norton & Boyd, 1978), I saw a studio portrait of her—startlingly out of place among the photographs of imposing mountain landscapes. The text explained that Isabella Bird, in November, 1873, had ridden on horseback from Estes Park to Colorado Springs, then back through South Park to Denver: a 500 mile junket primarily through uninhabited wilderness. Alone. Anyone who knows this route—rugged even today, some of it negotiable only by jeep—and who is familiar with the treachery of Colorado winter weather, would be impressed. No one, in fact, from that day to this has duplicated her feat. I searched the photography: disciplined white hair, placid face, somber garments, circles of flesh. I became intrigued. Who was this woman?

Other writers have been intrigued as well. Isabella Bird is the focus of chapters in several books on Victorian travellers; she is the subject of Pat Barr's (1970) detailed biography, *A Curious Life for a Lady;* she is a character in Caryl Churchill's (1982) *Top Girls;* and, after the lapse of a century, eight of her travel books have been reissued.

Pat Barr's biography with its clever title, *A Curious Life for a Lady,* is highly readable, but my interest in Isabella Bird differs from hers: I want to focus upon the choices that Bird made in order to become an unconventional traveller. Isabella Bird's story is even more exceptional when one remembers that neither her family nor Victorian patriarchal society encouraged her to pursue her interests. On the contrary, the weight of their tacit opposition was a burden she carried all her life. Her attraction for me is precisely in that she overcame the strictures of her family and of society.

Her isolation from a life of adventure was as total as if she were immured in a windowless cell built of heavy sand bags. That she had an operation for the removal of a spinal tumor when she was eighteen and years later had additional surgery on her back makes her achievements even more remarkable. But this ailment, paradoxically, aided her escape from her internment—which is not too severe a word. Her travels began in her search for health. Her unreliable health, in fact, provided her with the rationalization that she needed in order to travel, for she was never able to accept her unusual nature and the freedom that it required. She was deeply conflicted between her unacknowledged anger at being so repressed—her severe depression is a symptom of this anger turned upon herself—and guilt that she could not be the nonassertive, pleased-with-a-life-of-service person that gratified her sister.

The release that Isabella Bird experienced away from British and upper-middle class society is an indication that only in such circumstances was she able to reconcile the anger and the guilt in her personality. Significantly her nervous symptoms—depression, insomnia and headaches—disappeared when she was in the wilderness. My interest in writing her biography is in highlighting the decisions she made that finally enabled her to satisfy the demands of her rebellious nature.

Feminist scholars and critics, Adrienne Rich (1976, 1979), Nancy Chodorow (1978), Sandra M. Gilbert and Susan Gubar (1979), Carol Gilligan (1982), and Carolyn G. Heilbrun, have made us aware of the many aspects of a woman's experience in life and in literature that have not been previously considered. I am indebted to them and in particular to Heilbrun's (1988) brilliant book, *Writing a Woman's Life,* in which she poses these questions:

> there still exists little organized sense of what a woman's biography or autobiography should look like. Where should it begin? With her birth, and the disappointment, or reason for no disappointment, that she was not a boy? Do we then slide her into the Freudian family romance, the Oedipal configuration; if not, how do we view the childhood? And now that interest in the pre-Oedipal period has been so vigorously revived by French and American feminists, how closely do we look at that period? What, in short, is the subject's relation—inevitably complex—with her mother? The relation with the father will be less complex, clearer in its emotions and desires, partaking less of either terrible pity or binding love. How does the process of becoming, or failing to become, a sex object operate in the woman's life; how does she

> cope with the fact that her value is determined by how attractive men find her? If she marries, why does the marriage fail, or succeed? . . . What of women friends, of middle age, or of active old age? None of these questions has been probed within the context of women's as yet unnarrated lives, lives precisely *not* those that convention, romance, literature, and drama have, for the most part, given us. (p. 27)

My biography of Isabella Bird discusses these aspects of her life.

Certainly on the surface nothing foretold Isabella Bird's unlikely career. In fact, there was little of hope or of promise in what had become a woefully exiguous life. Isabella Bird had been born a frail child with a spinal ailment that plagued her all her years. In addition, it seems clear, her capacity to drink deeply of life was so hedged with restrictions, with prohibitions, with awareness of the needs of the less fortunate, that ordinary, everyday life itself became virtually intolerable. Until middle age she was a semi-invalid—at times requiring steel braces even to lift her head. She had twice been to America and in pursuit of health had taken a voyage to the Mediterranean (by way of New York!), but she had returned to England with the same backaches, headaches, and lassitude.

Isabella Bird, who was born in 1831, suffered the usual impediments that gender imposed in English Victorian society. To be submissive, self-effacing, and content with the sedentary life were particularly grievous for Isabella Bird, for unacknowledged by herself she had the desire for adventure, the fearlessness, and the curiosity that society usually associates with the male. She suffered also the expectations and strictures of an Evangelical upbringing. In many ways she was the stolid product of that Evangelical training: teaching Sunday School, writing hymns, organizing philanthropies, exercising self-denial, experiencing guilt if she read even Milton on Sunday, and eventually establishing hospitals. She had been schooled to deny any tendency towards self-indulgence, that is, anything that she might have wanted to do for her own pleasure or well-being.

Her mother's lifelong habit was her model: winter and summer Dora Bird rose before it was light to have a longer time for her morning devotions; she rose when sick; she rose even on her deathbed. To care for oneself was a form of indulgence. Bird's austere upbringing taught her to be dismayed at the promptings of her own nature, to view whatever she wanted to do as a fault she must labor to overcome. Such training made Isabella Bird feel it was necessary to justify herself. She wrote after she had undergone surgery for removal of a spinal tumour, "I feel as if my life were spent in the very ignoble occupation of taking care of myself" (Anna M. Stoddart, 1908, p. 57). That she did finally succeed in choosing the highly unconventional travel that gave meaning to her life is an indication of her curiosity, of her courage, and of the strength of the drive for expression within her.

Only when Isabella Bird made the choices that enabled her to express this adventurous side of her nature did all symptoms disappear. She was capable in her middle and late years of incredible physical exertion and hardship, and she then was, as she described herself, a woman with an "up-to-anything and free-legged air" (Pat Barr, 1970, p. 13).

At age forty-three Isabella Bird made a series of decisions. The one that had the most far-ranging consequences seemed at the time, as such things often do, almost trivial. It is about these decisions that I shall write, for it was by making these choices that Isabella Bird found her vocation: a vocation available to her, it must be underscored, because she had already made the choice to be single. In rejecting marriage, in refusing the "heterosexual plot"—the one option open to Victorian young ladies—Bird had created the condition necessary for her to be herself. She had refused to make a man the center of her life, turning down proposals from at least two suitors. In a society that gave a pejorative cast to the word "spinster"—a 17th century legal term denoting an unmarried state—making an aspersion of spinsterhood was a brave decision.

The choices she made were on yet another voyage to attain health and to alleviate her gloom that "this is such an aimless life" (Barr, 1970, p. 20). She was circling the globe—Australia, New Zealand, California. She had left New Zealand still a semiinvalid. Indeed she was in a sorry state, suffering not only ennui, but also severe headaches, backaches, neuralgia, sleeplessness, nervousness, exhaustion, and a paralyzing depression. The voyage had not been a success. As she was to discover, it was not travel itself that she craved, but travel away from the stultifying conventions society imposed.

In setting forth from Liverpool, Isabella Bird was making the choice that would enable her to become an autonomous woman; however, parting from her younger sister, Hennie, had been painful. Hennie was the only family she had, their father dead 16 years, their mother 7. The bond between the two sisters was the explanation that Bird gave for her single state: "He [Mr. Wilson who had just proposed] was a splendid-looking fellow and what I might have said if it had not been for *you* [Hennie] I don't know" (Barr, 1970, p. 47).

That Isabella's bond to Hennie was close, intense, and carried the cargo of her heart was true. Hennie was also single. (Bird did marry but only after Hennie's death. During the five years of her marriage until her husband's death she did not travel.) Hennie was Bird's intellectual equal. For instance, she taught herself Hebrew, Latin, and Greek—the better to understand the Bible—but she had a more compliant nature and a more devout character than her older sister. Isabella Bird compared herself unfavorably to Hennie and wished that she, like Hennie, might be content with the Sunday School classes, the tending to the poor, the quiet friendships, and the sketching of familiar scenes, that sufficed for Hennie. Hennie might be Penelope waiting at home, but what needs to be emphasized is that Hennie gave Bird the center she required in order to roam. The two sisters loved and encouraged one another, each giving to the other the support each needed to be herself.

Wherever Isabella Bird traveled she wrote to Hennie letters of extraordinary detail, written with such frequency one wonders she had time for anything else. Her ink and papers were always with her and no sooner was she settled than out they came. She wrote with wonderful freshness and observation, doing her best to describe as fully as possible everything that happened to her. She was, in putting words to paper, exercising a control over the flux of her life; she was discovering in writing, as other women have, the need to make a narrative of her life. Virginia Woolf has said that nothing was real until she wrote it down. The avidity, the tenaciousness of Bird's writing suggests that she too was making her life "real."

On the voyage, Bird's spirits had undergone a sharp change 2 days from Auckland, when the *Nevada* steamed headfirst into a hurricane, a hurricane so severe that the captain later declared it almost "boxed the compass;" the hurricane leveled the ocean, obscured the night, day, sea, sky, and horizon—all was intense black—and its winds made a constant piercing shriek unheard before. The *Nevada* was a steamer of the paddle-wheel type: old and decrepit. When it rained, meals were eaten in waterproofs and rubber shoes because the deck above leaked. Its ancient belabored engines lost their boiler tubes and the entire superstructure listed more and more to port. The unseaworthy boat was one peril, the hurricane was another. Both hazards dispelled her ennui. Even when the ailing engines stalled completely in the Tropic of Capricorn and the *Nevada* sat there limp and sizzling, Bird helped to shape the activities of the day: reading aloud *Idylls of the King,* playing chess, checkers, and quoits for exercise, taking turns fanning and nursing a stricken passenger, writing letters, and conversing. She was alert with, she confided, the youthful vigor of a girl of 21. Bird thrived, and in a revealing paragraph wrote:

> It is to me like living in a new world, unfettered, so full of interest that one grudges being asleep; and, instead of carrying cares and worries and thoughts of the morrow to bed with one to keep one awake, one falls asleep at once to wake to another day in which one knows that there can be nothing to annoy one—no door bells, no "Please mems," no dirt, no bills, no demands of any kind, no vain attempts to overtake all one knows one should do. Above all, no nervousness, and no conventionalities, no dressing. It sounds a hideously selfish life. (Stoddart, 1908, pp. 79–80)

To enjoy herself away from the petty, suffocating demands of her middle-class English life was—one notes that Evangelical training—"hideously selfish."

Bird had been on the high seas for 6 months when, in January 1873, the *Nevada* steamed into Honolulu harbor. She had not planned to stop in the Sandwich Islands (as Hawaii was then called), but to push on to San Francisco. The only other woman passenger, a Mrs. Dexter, was traveling with her grown son who had had a lung hemorrhage shortly after the *Nevada* left New Zealand. All the other passengers had taken turns caring for him, and it was agreed that if the young man were to live he would need care and attention in Honolulu. Mrs. Dexter was timid about disembarking alone and had asked Isabella Bird if she would stay with her. Bird had agreed. Oahu from a distance with barren grey peaks was a disappointment, but as the boat entered the harbor it was a colorful scene;

> We looked down from the towering deck on a crowd of two or three thousand people. . . . Such rich brown men and women they were, with wavy shining black hair, large, brown, lustrous eyes, and rows of perfect teeth. (Isabella Bird, 1985, pp. 14–15)

> Outside this motley, genial picturesque crowd about 200 saddled horses were standing, each with the Mexican saddle. . . . Every now and then a flower-wreathed Hawaiian woman . . .sprang on one of these animals astride, and dashed along the road at full gallop, sitting on her horse as square and easy as a hussar. (Bird, 1985, p. 16)

> The women seemed perfectly at home in their gay, brass-bossed, high peaked saddles, flying along astride, bare-footed, with their orange and scarlet riding dresses . . . a bright kaleidoscopic flash of bright eyes, white teeth, shining hair. (Bird, 1985, p. 22)

Isabella Bird's attitude towards the native population is an abrupt and sympathetic contrast to Victorian empire builders, missionaries, explorers, and other travelers who shared an assumption that they were of a higher class, that natives were to be saved and to be made like the English. She was not only observant of the natives but admiring: she did not have the prejudice of those English like Mr. Podsnap who felt contemptuous of others, or of those who were bent on converting the heathen into Christians. She asked, "But where were the hard, angular, careworn, sallow, passionate faces of men and women, such as form the majority of every crowd at home, as well as in America and Australia?" (Bird, 1985, p. 15). She continued in a pertinent statement: "The conditions of life must surely be easier here, and people must have found rest from some of the burdensome conventionalities" (Bird, 1985, 15). The "burdensome conventionalities" were an oppressive weight to Bird, and in part the escape from those onerous duties gave the nonEnglish peoples their appeal. Bird was particularly struck by the behavior of the women and later she wrote:

> Used to the down-trodden look and harassed, care-worn faces of the over-worked women of the same class at home and in the colonies, the laughing, careless faces of the Hawaiian women have the effect upon me of a perpetual marvel. (Bird, 1985, 181)

Nothing of the superior, of the condescending, of the take-me-as-the-model in Bird's attitude—an attitude even more remarkable in the light of the

Evangelical zeal for missions. Recall the character of St. John Rivers in *Jane Eyre,* a drawn from life Evangelical.

The *Nevada* was to be in port for only a few days and was then to toil on to California. Two of the men on board who were continuing the voyage were going to hire a carriage to drive to the Nuuanu escarpment. Would Miss Bird care to accompany them? Yes. A small incident, but recall that she was disembarking only because of Mrs. Dexter. One of the passengers offered to take Mrs. Dexter and her son in charge and to arrange for Miss Bird's room at the hotel. Mrs. Dexter assured Miss Bird that she would be comfortable. Notice that Isabella Bird preferred to explore far more than she preferred the conventional: accompanying Mrs. Dexter, arranging for a room, seeing what the hotel was like, unpacking. Under these halcyon skies, Bird could discard the self-sacrificing, self-effacing role and, assuring herself that Mrs. Dexter was well looked after, go off to the new and the unknown; this choice allowed a healthy selfishness to be asserted, a choice impossible in that "dim, pale island," as she called Great Britain. Bird was on her way back to the hotel when friends approached her and

> told me that a lady friend of theirs, anxious for a companion, was going to the volcano on Hawaii, that she was a most expert and intelligent traveller, that the *Kilauea* would sail in two hours, that unless I went now I should have no future opportunity during my limited stay on the islands, that Mrs. Dexter was anxious for me to go, that they would more than fill my place in my absence . . . that in short I *must* go, and they would drive me back to the hotel to pack! The volcano is still a myth to me, and I wanted to "read up" before going. (Bird, 1985, p. 29)

Notice the rapidity with which the decision was made as well as the almost breathless quality of the letter. Her one regret, other than leaving Mrs. Dexter, was that she was not able to study about volcanoes or about the big island of Hawaii before embarking. She had no hesitation in making this choice. Her eager interest in the natural world instantly impelled her to agree. Having only 2 hours to get ready, traveling with a total stranger, going to an area about which she knew nothing, with no prior arrangements made—all these were insignificant in the face of the opportunity to see more of the world.

On board she noticed as had Mark Twain a few years earlier "that there were very few trunks and portmanteaus, but that the after end of the saloon was heaped with Mexican saddles and saddlebags, which I learned too late were the essential gear of every traveller on Hawaii" (Bird, 1985, p. 31). Miss Karpe, whose desire for a traveling companion was the reason for Bird's taking this unexpected trip to Hawaii, organized the expedition to the Anuenue Falls. The narrow track led in and out of the stream and the horses stumbled from one rock to the next. When she returned to Hilo—no hotels, visitors stayed with local residents and Bird and Karpe were at the home of the local sheriff, Lawrence Severns—sore, tired, her back in an agony, she feared that she would have to forgo the morrow's outing to the volcano, for she refused to be carried by litter.

Here was Isabella Bird returned from the outing to the Falls, her back crippled, unable to get off the following day to Kilauea crater. Mr. Severns suggested that she do as the native Hawaiian ladies do, use a Mexican saddle and ride astride, and he saddled a horse to try it out. That a lady did not ride astride, but rode sidesaddle, was a truth universally acknowledged. Sidesaddle a lady's limbs were effectively covered and her skirts could billow demurely. Astride was unheard of. It was not done. Normally it was not even mentioned as a possibility.

> It was only my strong desire to see the volcano which made me consent to a mode of riding against which I have so strong a prejudice, but the result of the experiment is that I shall visit Kilauea thus or not at all. (Bird, 1985, p. 43)

This is the pivotal decision. Bird allies herself with her sister and their conservative, high-minded friends: "a mode of riding against which I have so strong a prejudice." But the bedrock of convention yields to curiosity: "my strong desire to see the volcano." This decision was the watershed of her life. Astride, she had no pain; astride, she could gallop up and down hills; astride, she could ride with the mad abandon, with the reckless energy for which her nature had been starved.

The immediate result of this decision was the need for clothes—she could not ride astride without covering her legs. For this expedition she wore a borrowed riding costume, furnishing, she said, "the grotesque" element (Bird, 1985, p. 46). She quickly stitched light flannel bloomers, like Turkish harem pants, ending in a frill at the ankle, over which she wore a loose skirt—her Bloomer Suit, she called it, attire that was a step away from convention, a step towards comfort and freedom.

The next morning the party of three started out, Isabella Bird, Miss Karpe on a sidesaddle, and the native guide Upa who set off at a full gallop. Bird clutched the horn of the saddle, the horse without guidance careered along the trail, every corner a terror, and stopped abruptly forcing her to grasp the mane to prevent being pitched over his head—to the immense amusement of a group of native women. The ignoble start was quickly corrected. Soon she wrote:

> Existence was a luxury, and reckless riding a mere outcome of the animal spirits of horses and riders, and the *thud* of the shoeless feet as the horses galloped over the soft grass was sweeter than music. I could hardly hold my horse at all and down hills . . . over knife-like ridges . . . and along side-tracks we rode at full gallop. (Bird, 1985, pp. 204–205)

> We rode widly and recklessly, galloping down steep hills . . . and putting our horses to their utmost speed. (p. 207)

> It was a joyously-exciting day, and I was galloping down a grass hill at a pace which I should not have assumed had white people been with me . . . and

> on coming to the top of a hill [we] put [our] horses into a gallop, and we all rode down at a tremendous, and, as I should have once though, a breakneck speed, when one of the women patted me on the shoulder, exclaiming, "mai-kai! mailai! *paniola* [cowboy! cowboy!]!" (pp. 218–219)

This from a woman whose spine was too weak to support her head! The contrast is striking when she returned to the luxuries of the recently built hotel in Honolulu and wrote: "The hotel is pleasant, and Mrs. D.'s presence makes it sweet and homelike; but in a very few days I have lost much of the health I gained on Hawaii" (p. 170). Bird was on the cusp of awareness, just beginning to recognize what it was her spirit required.

A packet of letters from Hennie forwarded from San Francisco prompted another choice: At once she decided to investigate the leeward islands and to postpone departure for another 4 months. If she had not heard from Hennie she would have sailed for San Francisco on the homeward trek. Mrs. Dexter's son had recovered; she had heard from Hennie. Isabella Bird was free at last to acknowledge and to follow her own desires to explore, to go to those far-from-the-center-of-civilization places. She was free to do what *she* wanted to do. Out in the open her sense of well-being returned:

> This is the height of enjoyment in travelling. I have just encamped under a lauhala tree, with my saddle inverted for a pillow, my horse tied by a long lariat to a guava bush, my gear, my saddle-bags, and rations for two days lying about, and my saddle blanket drying in the sun. . . . Was there ever such an adventure? And Nature—for I have no other companion, and wish none—answers, "No." (Bird, 1985, p. 237)

Liberated from paralyzing convention, Isabella Bird was the ideal traveler and travel writer. She was an astute observer and recorder—of people—how they live, labor, and worship—of landscapes, flora, fauna, street scenes, architecture, festivals. Danger stimulated her. She was not insensible of risk, but the questionable engines of the *Nevada,* the "most severe hurricane that the captain had seen in 17 years" (Bird, 1985, pp. 7–8), the proximity of two live volcanoes, raging torrents, all quickened her.

> My eyes seek the dome-like curve of Mauna Loa . . . for it is as yet an unfinished mountain. It has . . . a pit of unresting fire on its side; it throbs, rumbles, and palpitates; it has sent forth floods of fire over all this part of Hawaii and at any moment it may be crowned with a lonely light, showing that its tremendous forces are again in activity. (Bird, 1985, p. 37)

That the mountain is in process, is alive, "for it is as yet an unfinished mountain," excited Bird: "It is most interesting to be in a region of such splendid possibilities" (Bird, 1985, p. 62).

In the moving reel of Isabella Bird's life I have, as it were, stopped the action, to frame in still life those decisions that enabled her to release the "tremendous forces" within her and to become the woman she was capable of being, to realize "such splendid possibilities."

Certainly the path she followed of traveling by the most primitive means in remote places—Hawaii, the Rocky Mountains, northern Japan, Malaya, Persia, Korea, Tibet, on the backs of horses or yaks or camels or elephants, of staying in native huts—away from hotels and resorts, was one that had no female precedent. For a woman, brought up as she had been, to make these arduous excursions driven only by curiosity and by a love of adventure, traveling neither in the wake of a husband nor in the wake of an empire, was in itself a remarkable event. She went on to write nine popular travel books and was the first woman elected to the Royal Geographic Society. I want to celebrate that she was able to overcome the oppressive limitations that Victorian society placed upon middle class women and that she made the choices that expressed her basic nature and that enabled her to "write her own script."

My interest in her is in how she was able to break through the many "Thou shall nots" to discover her unusual occupation. Hers was not a direct path. She had no encouragement, no female predecessors. Her first choice, of which she was completely unconscious would enable her to find her unorthodox calling, was to refuse the one option open to Victorian young ladies—to make a man the center of her life. She was well into middle age, suffering from a plethora of nervous and physical disorders, on yet another voyage for her health, when a series of seemingly small decisions led her to find out that what she enjoyed above all was being by herself in the wilderness and writing about what she saw and felt. Her headaches, insomnia, and apathy vanished, and instead of the pain-racked nervous wreck she had been, she had the vigor of a girl of 21 with an "up-to-anything and free-legged air" (Barr, 1970, p. 13).

REFERENCES

Barr, Pat. (1970). *A curious life for a lady*. New York: Doubleday.

Bird, Isabella L. (1985). *Six months in the Sandwich Islands*. Rutland, VT: Charles E. Tuttle. (Original work published 1875.)

Chodorow, Nancy. (1978). *The reproduction of mothering: Psychoanalysis and the sociology of gender*. Berkeley: University of California Press.

Churchill, Caryl. (1982). *Top girls*. London: Methuen.

Gilbert, Sandra M., & Gubar, Susan. (1979). *The Madwoman in the attic: The woman writer and the nineteenth-century literary imaginagion*. New Haven: Yale University Press.

Gilligan, Carol. (1982). *In a different voice: Psychological theory and women's development*. Cambridge, MA: Harvard University Press.

Heilbrun, Carolyn G. (1988). *Writing a woman's life*. New York: WW Norton.

Norton, Barbara, & Boyd. (1978). *Backroads of Colorado*. Chicago: Rand McNallly.

Rich, Adrienne. (1976). *Of woman born*. New York: WW Norton.

Rich, Adrienne. (1979). *On lies, secrets, and silence*. New York: WW Norton.

Stoddart, Anna M. (1908). *The life of Isabella Bird*. New York: EP Dutton.

Part 3
Purposes

Usually biographies are written about people who are well-known or considered unusual in some way. Feminist biographies also largely conform to this pattern.

Sociologists using biographical methods have different purposes; they could be characterized as having a greater interest in knowing about the fabric of social life itself, rather than in the lives of specific individuals. Feminist sociologists have found life history methods particularly sensitive to research into women's lives.

Anne-Kathrine Broch-Due discusses the interview process, which she uses as a basis for her own life history work, the two-way changes, for herself and for her informants. Ann Nilsen also works with the life history method, and writes about the contradictions involved in using biographic methods to make a sociology for women. Contradictions are especially clear in the area of preserving her informants' right to privacy while still using the information they give her to write about their lives.

Chapter 9

Reflections on Subjectivism in Biographical Interviewing: A Process of Change

Anne-Kathrine Broch-Due

INTRODUCTION

Writing a person's life history is most commonly associated with biographies of well-known individuals. But the biographic method based on telling and detailing people's lives—either part or the whole life history—has a long tradition in the social sciences. For sociological purposes it is possible to do research based on one life history, or to construct the life histories of a number of people concurrently and to work with them as a collection of parallel histories. An outstanding example of the life history approach is *The Polish Peasant* written by W. I. Thomas and Florian Znaniecki and published as early as 1927.

There has been an increased interest in the life course perspective over the last 10 to 15 years, and especially so in feminist research. One reason for this is a general feeling that important qualities of many people's lives (and emphatically of women's lives) have been excluded from representation in the main body of research. The use of methods incorporating biography may therefore be a way of broadening the base of feminist sociology.

As well as being popular for the reasons mentioned above, a working interest in the life story makes some common ground between traditions. This interest is a common point of departure for both the literary biographer and the writer of life histories. If they are writing about contemporary lives both may use the interview as a method; equally, both may be concerned with the historical circumstances in which their subject lived. There are differences, though, especially of purpose. Literary biographies are by and large concerned with making public the lives of people who are already "named" as unusual, and often are talented in some special way. The biography itself may be an aspect of their fame. For social scientists, their interest has to do with making public the fabric of social life itself and creating ways of understanding and describing what happens to people in the ordinary way of things. However, despite such differences, there are shared methods which are worth discussing. One of these is the process of interviewing. It is on the way that I see the interview within my own research that I concentrate in the following chapter, especially emphasizing the creative potential of both subjectivism and change.

THE QUALITATIVE RESEARCH INTERVIEW

In general, when doing qualitative research, the main purpose is to learn how individuals create meaning in their lives, how they create and interpret their lives given the material conditions in which they live. In other words, the purpose of this kind of sociology is to recognize and show the fabric of life, which often slips through the net in quantitative research. This purpose is especially the case when research is guided by a life-course approach.

We can define a qualitative research interview as an interview aiming to gather the interviewee's description of her life. The purpose of this is to interpret meaning in her description, and so to gain greater understanding about the happenings (the "phenomena") which she has related to the researcher. The qualitative research interview is different from the therapeutic interview in the sense that the former is not directed toward an explicit change of the interviewee's life situation. But, as I will argue later, change may unavoidably take place when using a qualitative research interview—both for the researcher and the interviewee—even it not intended.

POSITIVISM

In the positivist framework for research, professional researchers remove themselves from involvement in the "subject-matter" for the purpose of obtaining a picture of an objective reality. "Positivism sees what is studied as an 'object.' 'The subject' is the researcher, and she can stand back from the object/s of study (people), and look at it/them objectively and dispassionately" (Liz Stanley & Sue Wise, 1983, p. 194). Efforts to attain this goal of "pure science" have also been common among researchers using qualitative research interviews; this is all the more remarkable as they are aware of the impossibility of such a venture; avoiding criticism within the establishment may be one of the reasons for this.

One of the main features of positivist thought is its polarization of ideas into dichotomies, that is, the division of features of a situation into categories which are mutually exclusive, and which may never merge with each other. This method is reflected in the everyday thinking and language of Western countries and most significantly characterizes the positivistic theory of science through the division (for the purpose of analysis) of researcher-as-subject from the researcher-as-object, and separation of reason and emotion. Dichotomizing the world is itself a serious limitation for thought, but in addition it involves the problem of gender. The "rational, objective" side of the dichotomy is at the same time a characteristic of both "pure science" and traditionally ascribed masculine practices and values in Western societies.

There are very practical consequences that follow from the way the researcher sees herself in relation to the above position (see Liz Stanley's chapter, 11, for an elaboration on an alternative way of understanding analysis of social life). When two human beings meet to talk or have a conversation (and that is what qualitative interviewing is about) an objective, dispassionate researcher can hardly be seen as anything but a "myth." Correspondingly, whether the interviewee is seen as an object or a subject has consequences. The choice will have a great impact on the whole process of interviewing, the type of knowledge the researcher is able to get, and how the process of analysis and interpretation is viewed. What kind of information the researcher may obtain from the interview is part of this too.

The qualitative interview is a relation between two subjects. I will elaborate this point, and argue that this attitude can be a strength instead of a weakness in such an interview.

Researcher as Researcher Different from Researcher as Person

In positivism it is important to see the researcher as "a researcher" as different from the researcher as a person. I have never understood this transition or metamorphosis. When does it take place? Is it when you close the office door behind you and start to work on your research? Or is it a slowly happening process during the education and training to be a researcher? Of course, as a researcher you are influenced by your training and education. You work systematically, guided by rules, and using tools developed by the scientific community. But does this eliminate you as a person? Methodologically this separation, says David Bakan (1969): "differentiates between the man in his functioning as a scientist and in his functioning as a human being. This distinction is both unfortunate and unreal" (p. 51). On the contrary, he recommends the researcher be

> more aware of the factors associated with the knowledge-getting process. We need to become more aware of the operation of psychological and cultural

> factors in our own research operations, for they largely constitute the operations of our investigatory work. What we ordinarily call methodology needs to be expanded to include the culture and psychology of psychologists. (Bakan, 1969, p. 49)

I will expand Bakan's recommendation to include all social scientists as researchers, whether they are trained as psychologists, sociologists, or anthropologists.

The fact that positivism differentiates between the researcher as a researcher and as a person has important consequences. First, because the ideal researcher in the positivistic view is objective and dispassionate, emotions are by definition removed from her. Reason is the only available channel to facilitate understanding. On the basis of psychotherapy, Jette Fog (1985) discusses the unfortunate contradiction between reason and emotion within psychotherapy. She argues that reason and emotion are different but essential channels for understanding. This opens up the areas of intuitive and empathic modes of understanding. It means that instead of overlooking the influence of our emotions we have to be aware of them and add them to our methodological assets.

Secondly, even though in the positivist frame the researcher is known to be a particular subject, this subjectivity is not taken into account in the interview situation. There is a denial by omission of the fact that the researcher has a gender, belongs to a certain race, social class, and culture, and that all these as social facts have some influence on her research. My feeling is that social scientists should be the first to acknowledge these social influences on their work.

The Interviewee

In stark contrast with the way the researcher is conceptualized, the gender, race, social class, culture, and so on are seen as important features of the interviewee, but each of them is seen as an individual factor that can separately explain aspects of the issues involved; this again means a splitting up so that these characteristics are not seen as rooted within complex processes of interaction.

SHOWING THE CONNECTIONS

As an alternative to the traditional ideal of "valuefree, objective" science I place myself in the epistemological tradition that views knowledge as dependent on the knowing subject. I see the interview situation as a dialectical relation between two subjects: in other words, what has been defined as *intersubjectivity* (Marcia Westkott, 1979). Both the researcher and the interviewee are whole persons, where gender, race, social class, and culture are important social facts in the process of shaping their subjectivity; or, to put it another way, these facts have influenced their experience and their own interpretation of themselves in the process of shaping them as social persons. For the researcher this will involve *conscious subjectivity* as a part of the method. As Renate Duelli Klein (1983) has pointed out, conscious subjectivity must not be confused with uncritical acceptance of a person's statements.

Impact of a Life-Course Approach

Using a qualitative interview does not necessarily imply a life-course approach, but when it does time and space become crucial concepts. This may be the key to showing the positivist framework as absurd and inappropriate as a means of analyzing life experience. It makes visible the view that the construction of knowledge is dependent upon the subject.

A person's life history is a process or movement in a space-time location over a certain period. These are facts both for the researcher and the interviewees. By a life-course approach a person, a group of people, or an organization are followed over a certain time span. The focus in a life-course approach is on individuals' lives in their social context in a certain historical period. The individual life history is displayed between the framework of biographical time (age) and historical time (period). But the individual is not only a member of the large society. She belongs to many smaller collectives like the family, peer group, neighborhood, working place, and so forth. Norms and expectations toward these collectives may change over time and restructure these collectives themselves. In addition we can therefore also add family time, peer group time, and so on, to the analysis. The biological processes of maturing and aging take place within the complex interaction of these social, cultural, and historical conditions—conditions that themselves are changing and defined by their own time.

The timing of events and occurrences within these frames of reference is the main focus that structures the research of either an individual life history or many life histories put together (cohort analysis). While cohort analysis emphasizes the typicality of an event (i.e., first childbirth), the individual life history shows the variations. For the purpose of this article I will limit discussion to the life history.

The choice of interviews as a basis for life-history writing allows for emphasis to be given to the self-understanding of the interviewee: how she tells the reasons and interprets transitions and events in her own life. For instance, this may enable the researcher to find a way of describing how a particular person is able to make dramatic changes, compared to what is commonly expected, while another in a similar situation (as it seems when you watch it from outside) does not?

Through having a life-course approach guiding my research, it has been difficult not to be aware of my own life history as a specific time-space location: the specific historical and social circumstances that have framed my life and the interpretations and meanings I have drawn from them. I cannot separate myself as a person from my thinking as a researcher, therefore I have to be consciously aware of a two-way process in the interview situation, when the interviewee's life history is shaped as it is told; through the transformation of editing, and the construction of the written life histories; and at the end when doing the analysis of the life histories.

These questions of the way the writer/researcher relates to the person she is interested in, as a subject rather than a source of data, have a profound influence both on a literary biographer and a sociologist. Some problems however are different—in my research I write about living people and, because they have no personal protection regarding the use to which the research is put, it is important to hide their identity; anonymity is important, as distinct from a biography where the knowledge of the person's identity is an important aspect of the book, in relation to its commercial value (see Ann Nilson's chapter, 10 in this book).

Interview as a Process of Change

The process of qualitative interviewing and analyzing is a process of change on at least three different levels. First the interviewee is telling her life history or talking about important topics in her life. Second, the information collected in others' life stories will challenge the interviewer's view both professionally and personally and will initiate change. Third, the outcome of the two former levels of change is that qualitative interview as a research process in itself is also a process of change. Even though this aspect is commonly neglected in quantitative positivistic research, the possibility of change on the three levels will always be inherent. I have found however that this fact is difficult or impossible to overlook when I do qualitative interviews guided by a life-course perspective or a biographical approach. In a life-course approach the time dimension is present from the starting point of the project (the project design), throughout the whole research process of collecting "data," and in the process of analysis (diachronic data). This is quite different from the situation in which quantitative "data" is collected from only one point in time (synchronic data). I will discuss these levels of concern in more detail.

For the Interviewee. One of the main claims in traditional positivistic methodology has been the claim that data should be able to be reproduced. When it comes to qualitative interviews, it is impossible to attain intrasubjective reproduction of data. As the interview takes place, the interviewee will get new understandings about aspects of her life and perhaps create new meaning for herself. A told life history is at the same time an interpreted one. It is thereby impossible for another researcher to come back and get the same answers to the same questions.

This "therapeutic effect" is well known. New understanding and meaning for the interviewee about her own life also means another way of thinking about possibilities and action, because it is always *the last* interpretation about your life that counts—that lays the ground for the way the future is viewed. Choices, plans, and wishes a person has in the *present* are based upon her interpretation of her life story in the *past* and lay the ground for how possibilities are viewed in the *future*. Change can take place during the interview, but may not be evident until afterwards. Indeed, if reinterviewing does not take place this aspect may not be shown at all in the research.

By doing pilot interviews in my own project, working with high school students, I had the opportunity to see quite dramatic changes for one of the interviewees which were initiated by her telling her life story. In one pilot interview an 18-year-old high-school student was asked retrospectively questions about family relations, friends, school experiences, and prospective questions about the future. While she was talking about herself she suddenly stopped, and made surprised comments on her position (or the role she had played) in her family. Throughout the interview she had gotten a new understanding about her position in her family, especially her relationship to her father and the role she had played in the relationship between parents. On the same evening as the interview, she went home and told her mother that she no longer wanted to be a "nice and always helpful" daughter, and on the same evening she broke up her relationship with her boyfriend. Just talking about her life at greater length had dramatic consequences. Among others, Ann Oakley (1981) has described this kind of effect in her research.

Most people do not usually have the opportunity to talk about their daily lives without being disturbed or interrupted. This may be one reason why quite simply being in a situation talking about life or important aspects of life can in itself have therapeutic effects. When I started up my interviews with 55 high school students this also became evident. Instead of having to persuade them to participate, which was what I thought would be the situation, they were eager to line up and everybody wanted to be the first. One way of interpreting the willingness they showed to be interviewed is that they seldom had had the opportunity to talk about themselves to an adult or anybody else at length. This was confirmed when I asked them about it, and some of them told me so without me having to ask. These high school students also report the "therapeutic" effect of talking: "It's nice to be able to talk about my life;" "Now I remember a lot of things;" "This has made me think about a lot of things."

For the Researcher. I found that interviewing people about their life histories or writing a biography was also a process of expanding my own knowledge, and new knowledge was sometimes a challenge to the meanings I had made about myself and my own life. I could feel how the aspects of potential recognition or identification in the information can be experienced as threatening or provocative for the interviewer, especially a female interviewer working with women. Certainly it may imply reconsideration of her own way of living.

THE RESEARCH PROCESS

In the terms of an intersubjective approach, the interview is a mutual construction (by the researcher and the interviewee) of the interviewee's life history. The aspects of change that accompany this process turn the qualitative research interview itself into a process of change. As human beings have reflecting minds, new knowledge will continually influence the researcher, give rise to new ideas as themes for research and shape the direction of the research as it progresses. A research process guided by a conscious subjectivity can make openings for new knowledge.

CONCLUSION

In one sense, the researcher's influence on her field of research and vice versa is not a new topic in science; it belongs within the general discussion on positivism and objectivity in research. Feminist, social scientists have, especially in the 1980s, written detailed and concrete reports from their own research on how they got around this topic using different kinds of qualitative methods (for instance, Frigga Haug, 1985; Renate Duelli Klein, 1983; Ann Oakley, 1981).

In this chapter I have reflected on the use of qualitative research interviews as a particular kind of method and the aspects of change that this process involves. When research is guided by a life-course perspective, methodological problems focused in feminist work become central. Although the purpose of sociological research is different from that of literary biography as a genre, the issues discussed in this chapter can clearly be brought to bear on biographic work of all kinds.

REFERENCES

Bakan, David. (1969). *On method: Towards a reconstruction of psychological investigation.* San Fransisco: Jossey-Bass.

Duelli Klein, Renate. (1983). How to do what we want to do: Thoughts about feminist methodology. In Gloria Bowles & Renate Duelli Klein (Eds.), *Theories of women's studies.* London: Routledge & Kegan Paul.

Fog, Jette. (1985). Om den folsomme fornuft og den fornuftige folsomhed. Psykoterapi som erkjennelsesparadigme [About the sensitive reason and the reasonable sensitivity. Psychotherapy as a paradigm of acknowledgment]. *Psyke og logos, 1,* Dansk psykologisk Forlag.

Haug, Frigga. (1985). Memory-work. *Psyke & Logos, 1,* Dansk psykologisk Forlag.

Oakley, Ann. (1981). Interviewing women: A contradiction in terms. In H. Roberts (Eds.), *Doing feminist research.* London: Routledge & Kegan Paul.

Stanley, Liz & Wise, Sue. (1983). *Breaking out: Feminist consciousness and feminist research.* London: Routledge & Kegan Paul.

Thomas, W. I. & Znaniecki, F. (1927). *The Polish peasant.* New York: Alfred A. Knopf.

Westkott, Maria. (1979). Feminist criticism in the social sciences. *Harvard Educational Review, 49*(4), 422–30.

Chapter 10

Using Life Histories in Sociology

Ann Nilsen

The life-course approach in sociology encompasses a wide variety of methods, from strictly quantitative questionnaires that may be circulated to huge populations, to in-depth biographies of only one or two individuals. My concern in the following chapter will be with the *use* of biographies, or life histories, of living people for sociological purposes.

In contrast to most biographical work, when presenting a life history for research purposes it is usually crucial to keep the identity of the interviewee confidential. It is about the ethics surrounding the representation of the lives of "ordinary people" that I intend to write. The people themselves may well have no interest in becoming publicly "known" and certainly the life story is not published to reveal private information about a particular person. I would see the purpose behind the sociological interest in biography as having a double intent: first to gain a wider understanding of people's lives in a society and culture at a particular time; and second to place an individual at the center of that understanding, so that the particular society, at the time at which she lives, can be seen through her eyes and her understanding of it.

ETHICAL CONCERNS

When considering how to present the results of her work, for instance in an academic journal or as a dissertation, the researcher may know that her interviewees are not likely to read what she has written. This fact does not, however, give her complete freedom to present the interviewees in any manner she chooses. Not, at least, if ethical considerations are to be taken into account. Reflections on how to present a life history should perhaps also include thoughts on how the interviewee would react to the presentation—even if she is not likely to read it. If such thoughts are taken into account only in cases where the interviewee is going to read what has been written, it would then be reasonable to ask if the reflections being made are more of a *strategic* than an ethical kind, and further to ask with what kind of feminism would this be compatible.

Here, as in the stages mentioned above, researchers have found different solutions. Some choose to let their informants read reports or articles before they are published (Ken Plummer, 1983). This practice, however praiseworthy it may seem, is not without serious implications as there is reason to believe that some people are better able to articulate their potential disagreements to the presentation than others. Further, it may not be unrealistic to believe that this might lead to an underreporting of the lives of more privileged groups of people. W. Fuchs (1984) remarked that certain groups of people have more resources than others if they intend to stop a publication they think will have a harmful effect on them. His standpoint is not to leave the interviewees uninformed, but rather to give honest and straightforward information on what *kind* of work is to be published, and the *intention* of it (Fuchs, 1984, p. 302). He states further that such information might show the group of interviewees in question that social science is not only for "the others." By discussing the intentions of a particular research project with the informants involved and the different ways of presenting results, it may be possible to minimize the risks of people feeling "betrayed" through the process as it moves beyond their control.

INTERPRETATIONS

To take up the substantive issues always found within the interpretation of interview data, I will start by describing my own practice. At my first meeting with the interviewees I describe the purpose of my research and also make them familiar with the fact that their life history will be one of several in my study. Further, I tell them how this will have consequences for the way at least some of the material will be presented. These consequences are incurred after the interview is over—possibly quite a long time afterwards, and certainly, during the interview, the emphasis is on the uniqueness of that one informant's life history. Very many issues arise for feminists about what this means for themselves in relation to the women who have shared their life stories with them, and what it means for feminist knowledge.

Again following my own practice, I bring a number of the life histories together, and the focus changes from my involvement with the interpretation of a particular woman's life to a concern with common experiences. For me the purpose of this is that knowledge and insight could be gained which would serve the interests of women in general. I would not see such a way of using biographical material as objectifying women. Rather I would argue that such an approach is justified because of its potential to extend understanding of similarity and difference between women in particular life circumstances. The next step in the process would be a rereading of each life history with a view to responding to it in a more aware way, informed by familiarity with several of the histories as a group.

However, questions always arise about the extent to which any researcher is able to relate to the realities of her informants. The issue of betrayal mentioned previously—in the sense of the ethical relationship a researcher has with each individual interviewee—is relevant again here in a political sense. The history of social research does reveal occasions where people have felt betrayed and presented in an inappropriate way in biographical (and other!) research (see R. F. Ellen, 1984; L. Langness & G. Frank, 1985). Because one must take for granted that researchers do not intentionally present their informants in such ways, it is crucial to give thorough consideration to this in the various phases of the research process. For a sociologist the issue becomes particularly clear when writing about people whose lives are lived in a context which differs very much from the researcher's own. For instance when a white, middle class researcher collects life histories of unemployed black women, the difference in status and background is such that the research—if ethical and political considerations were not taken seriously—could do injustice to the group involved. In anthropology, where material differences between researchers and informants are often explicit, the problems become overt. (For a further discussion on the issue in relation to anthropology, see Langness & Frank, 1985, p. 134–136.)

Another version of the dilemma might occur where the researcher's interpretation—from a theoretical or political standpoint—is in conflict with the interviewee's definition of the situation at an individual level. Janet Finch (1984) described such a situation from one of her research projects. She felt that if she were to refer her findings from an individual level only, they could be used "to undermine the interests of wives and mothers generally, if not necessarily the specific people she had interviewed" (p. 83). This would be a somewhat different version of the betrayal theme. As Finch states, it would be betrayal on a different level from the personal—it would mean betrayal in a more collective sense of the term, by "undermining the interests of women in general" (p. 85). In short, where the researcher has life histories from a group of people being faithful to each individual's definition of a situation can be difficult because the picture they present collectively may be in conflict with the perspective of individuals.

Leaving Analysis Until the End: The Difficulties

By analyzing and making theories and various kinds of general statements, the researcher acts within some kind of theoretical framework. In my own practice, I see this as putting on "spectacles" through which I interpret the personal story told by the interviewee. This is the case whatever group of people or single person is interviewed. In doing this I see myself operating at a different level of interpretation. The theoretical approach on this level may either come as a result of the reading of the life histories, or be chosen by the researcher beforehand. In the case of the latter, one usually turns the life history into a *case study;* the former deals with it as a *case history*.

As has already been discussed, the information generated when several life histories—or biographies—are taken as a group, amounts to a type of knowledge which is no longer authentic at a personal level. At this point, depending on the approach to and the use of the material, there is a danger of rendering the interviewees silent (see B. Alver, 1990, Fuchs, 1984, Plummer, 1983, Florian Znaniecki, 1934). The main problem here is the fact that interpretations are on two different levels, and in the process of making personal information comprehensive in sociological terms there is a danger of objectifying the individual. Because this is at the core of the problem area addressed here, it requires some elaboration.

When interviewing with a life history perspective, it is the *uniqueness* of one individual life which is conveyed to the researcher. When several life histories are collected for the purpose of generating knowledge on a different level, the uniqueness of the one will eventually have to disappear, and she becomes part of an aggregate or a larger group. The question is whether this can be understood, as objectifying. If so, how can this be avoided, or at least justified by the purpose for which it is undertaken? Further aspects of the individual life histories may disappear for a very different reason: concern for the anonymity of particular interviewees in the published research. In order to keep the identity of interviewees confidential, it is usually necessary to change the names of people and places. One may also have to alter dates when events took place, and so forth. As Ken Plummer (1983) remarks, in doing this the authenticity of the story is diminished. In making decisions on how far one can go in this respect without altering the story completely, the interests of the interviewee play a part. In some circumstances, it could do much harm, not only to her, but also to other people close to her, to have her life story published in a recognizable way.

When interviewing women for my own research project, I have found that they are more concerned about the hurt they may inflict on others than about themselves, if their identity is not kept confidential. During the interviewing, sensitive information about persons, relationships, emotions, and situations is revealed. Such information need not always be part of the published story. Sometimes, however, it will be necessary to give account of this too, in order to understand both the person and her times more fully. For instance, the types of emotional conflicts that women have in the Western societies at this specific period in history may be different from those women had in the same places 50 years ago, and may be different again from those experienced in other parts of the world. When such issues are described and the researcher has only one or just a few interviewees, she has to strike a balance between the demand for authenticity and the interviewee's need to stay anonymous.

CONCLUSION

The claim of presenting an authentic and "true" story—with respect to people's interpretation of situations they have experienced—is not unproblematic. The focus on postmodern theories of social sciences in this decade, especially, puts the debate of subjectivity versus objectivity, fact versus fiction, and absolutism versus relativism firmly on the agenda (see Sandra Harding, 1986). Rather than focusing on the authenticity of the life histories with respect to exact dates, places, names, and so forth, it would perhaps be better to give more attention to "authenticity of meaning"—that is, to see one's primary goal as being faithful to the informants' "truths," to make efforts to understand the informants' "definition of the situation."

This examination of the use of biographical methods shows the split loyalties a feminist can experience when writing for the academic world. It shows the necessity for protecting the anonymity of the women who participate in research, and the consequences this has for the ways their lives may eventually be presented.

REFERENCES

Alver, Bente Gullveig. (1990). *Creating the source through folkloristic field-work: A personal narrative*. Forthcoming in the series: *Folklore Fellows Communications, no. 246*.

Ellen, R. F. (1984). *Ethnographic research*. New York: Academic Press.

Finch, Janet. (1984). It's great to have someone to talk to: The ethics and politics of interviewing women. In Colin Bell & Helen Roberts (Eds.), *Social researching. Politics, problems, practice*. London: Routledge & Kegan Paul.

Fuchs, W. (1984). *Biographische forschung* [Biographical Research]. Opladen: Westdeutscher Verlag.

Harding, Sandra. (1986). *The science question in feminism*. Ithaca, NY: Cornell University Press.

Langness, L., & Frank, G. (1985). *Lives. An antropological approach to biography*. NOVATO, CA: Chandler & Sharp Publishers.

Plummer, Ken. (1983). *Documents of life*. London: Allen & Unwin.

Znaniecki, Florian. (1934). *The method of sociology*. New York: Rhinehard.

Part 4
Writers

What does it matter who the writer is, how she changes in the process of writing the biography, and what she feels for her subject? What is special for a woman writer when her subject is a woman? What are the sources available to biographers of women, and is information becoming more accessible?

A certain momentum of interest has developed in biographies of women, especially when they are written by women. This section examines some of the fertile personal and political ground from which feminist enthusiasm for writing biography might spring. Liz Stanley examines the interweaving of abstract theory with the concrete in the biographical process. Margaret Forster discusses her own "life" of Elizabeth Barrett Browning. Elizabeth Crawford writes about the "sources" from her experience of dealing in women's books and documents.

Chapter 11

Process in Feminist Biography and Feminist Epistemology

Liz Stanley

Dear Diary:

Talking about my work on Hannah Cullwick's diaries at the summer school a few weeks ago, I was asked if I liked her (with the implication, I thought, that I *did* like her). I said no I didn't, indeed I often but not always disliked her (or at least some facets of her character), but that I did *respect* her a good deal. I shocked the inquirer, her response suggested. She didn't seem to think it 'proper' in feminist terms to produce a biography of a woman you didn't like, nor, she said, would the product actually be satisfactory, "a good biography." I'm glad I'm an improper feminist then, for I can't help but think respect is a jolly sight more important than liking in coming to grips with someone's character and behaviour. But my reply conveyed only one aspect of how I feel and think about it. I should have also added that nonetheless I spent some years "in love with" Hannah; but that anyway the roots of my interest lay not in this but in the problematics "she," my construction of Hannah out of her own highly motivated writings, pose for how to understand and engage with other complex human beings and their lives: the root problematic of all social life as well as a crucial if often subterranean topic for social science inquiry and theorising. The inquirer and the others were I think happier when I talked about more obvious links between "my life" and "Hannah's life" in class terms & so on; but the changes that this experience, "editing HC's diaries," produced in my life it seems to me now are located in the "mind" aspects, the intellectual problematics. (Diary, 26 July, 1988)

Serendipitously, in December 1982 I was asked to write a short account of the "life and works" of Olive Schreiner for a book on feminist theorists of the past (Dale Spender, 1983; Liz Stanley, 1983). Quite literally this changed my life, by initiating a process which confirmed my existing reader's interest—preoccupation almost—with diaries, letters, autobiographies and biographies, and also transformed it into a feminist sociological analytical concern with them. I became increasingly aware both of the need for feminists to develop an analytic approach to *reading* or *consuming* such textual sources, and for feminists researching auto/biographies to become analytically aware of the process of *writing* or *producing* them. I also became centrally aware, from my own experience, of how close the links are between the life or autobiography of biographers, and the written biographies they produce (for one instance of this see Stanley, 1987a).

In this chapter I discuss my concern with the production rather than consumption side of feminist auto/biography (although in Liz Stanley, in press, I do discuss reading such materials). I begin by explaining in more detail the developments and shifts in my own work as a feminist sociologist (rather than historian or literature specialist, the two academic disciplines more closely associated with biography) involved with 'writing feminist biography.' This is then followed by a more focused discussion of what might be the elements of a distinctly feminist approach to auto/biography production and writing. I conclude with a briefer look at the implications of this for an understanding of the nature of a feminist theory of *knowledge,* for a feminist *epistemology,* and its relationship to feminist ways of living and *being,* to feminist *ontology*.

A BIOGRAPHER'S AUTOBIOGRAPHY

Autobiographies come in many shapes and sizes. What appears in this section is a highly selective and glossed autobiographically oriented account of some of my own developing (hopefully) and changing (certainly) practices as a feminist biographer. It is therefore not to be seen as the complete facts, but as an account that is directed toward a particular set of purposes (as indeed all accounts, autobiographical and other, always are)—purposes which are not wholly recoverable within the account itself. However, the sections of the chapter that follow this one focus on these other elements, thus making them accountable to you the reader. In these I argue that narratively structured auto/biographical accounts and analytically structured theoretical accounts are in fact highly similar; what follows in this section is thus to be read as analysis and theory, as much as description and narrative.

When I was a very little girl and my Mum was getting me off to sleep, I would read haltingly aloud to her (as she dozed off beside my bed) the lives of kings, queens, and famous men and women from my small store of books. My interest in and enjoyment of auto/biography is a very longstanding one. However, it was because of my feminist and sociological concern with epistemology—with theories of knowledge and its making—as a political phenomenon through and through that I became *analytically* interested in diaries, letters, biographies, and autobiographies.

The first step was through reading the early and mid-Victorian diaries of Arthur Munby edited by Derek Hudson (1972), in which small selections from the diaries of Hannah Cullwick appear in editorial passages, as do many more mentions of Hannah in Munby's diaries. I was immediately intrigued, in part because the tale of upper class Munby and decidedly lower class Hannah (who was employed as a domestic servant) was echoed by a similar cross-class relationship in my own working class family history, but more importantly because, in reading these three voices a clash of knowledges was half-revealed. I read Munby's diaries all one fascinated night and I then wanted to know much more about both him and Hannah. I ended by spending some 4 years of my life transcribing and editing the voluminous diaries of Hannah Cullwick (Stanley, 1984a), but also in responding to these, not as repositories of alternative *truths* to those advanced by Munby and by Derek Hudson, but rather as alternative and competing *constructions* designed for a purpose (which changed over time).

It is important to emphasize this point, as editors of diaries in general are not infrequently assumed to be treating the diary form as transparently objective, a flat surface of visible fact, as has happened with my own work on Hannah's diaries (Julia Swindells, 1986). My project was a different one: Firstly, to ensure that the Cullwick diaries appeared in print, for then and now these seem to me almost unique—within them a thoroughly working class woman, a domestic servant of the 1850s, 1860s, and 1870s, speaks and writes in her own voice; secondly and relatedly, to recognize the textual interconnections of the Cullwick with the Munby diaries and to emphasize that both used their diaries to promote a highly particular view of the relevancies of the—very different—social milieux in which each took part. Working on the two sets of diaries brought home to me, as an editor and commentator, in a very immediate way that the diary form, although apparently descriptive and written in the immediacy of the moment, is in fact as selective and as highly glossed a theoretical formulation of 'a life' as any autobiography, biography, or piece of formal theorizing. Moreover, although in the manuscript diaries Hannah's own voice speaks, I was well aware that the published version of her diaries, necessarily presenting selections from the manuscripts, is actually my construction of what this "voice" is. So I tried to provide readers with an account of the assumptions, convictions, and views that underpinned the selections made.

Biographers and other historians deal centrally with time, or rather with time-travel, for theirs is the task of grappling with both the dislocations and the symmetries between "then" and "now;" I would argue that a good biography is one which avoids temporal chauvinism but nonetheless conveys the relevancies of its small slice of then for the now its readers are living through. However, this is by no means a straightforward business. Indeed its complexities can take unexpected and sometimes unresolvable forms.

Lives, in whatever form they are written and published, typically contain photographs of their subjects. The ways in which photographs (or other visual presentations of a self) help structure the ways in which we read and understand character in auto/biography are seriously underdiscussed (although see Roland Barthes, 1980; John Berger, 1972; Erving Goffman, 1976; Susan Sontag, 1978; Jo Spence, 1986). For instance, the lives of Bloomsbury in general and Virginia Woolf in particular seem to me highly influenced by the photographic records published in various writings about Bloomsbury denizens; I can't help but wonder whether the history of Marxism would have been different had Karl Marx been a whizened and pinched figure rather than leonine, as in the view that is characteristically presented of him.

Both the influence of, and the temporal complexities embedded in, photographic views of biographical subjects were raised for me in making selections of photographs to appear in the published Cullwick diaries (as I discuss in detail in Liz Stanley, 1987b). Some of the photographs Hannah had had taken for Munby are, in late 20th century terms, sexual ones involving some degree of bodily nakedness, in particular showing her breasts. Yet the leitmotif both of Hannah's life and of her relationship with Munby was work, not sex howsoever defined. Moreover, as both their diaries suggest, nakedness was precisely that for them, not any erotically charged nudity. However and in some contrast, other photographs exist which show the transformations of dress that Hannah engaged in. There is one particular photograph of her in a lady's evening dress which seemed entirely innocuous to my eyes initially, but I later became aware that it was highly erotically charged for both of them. This was in part because of the transformations Hannah engaged in (of dress but also of character, from woman to lady), but also because it revealed her upper arms. I faced a puzzle. Should I select the "erotic" photographs which I was under some subtle pressure to include, knowing that readers would see and interpret them as sexually titillating, or should I instead select the "innocuous" photograph, knowing as I did its charged erotic meaning for Hannah and for Munby, so exposing them in their own terms and values although not those of contemporary readers? Whichever I chose, ethical issues would remain, but also intellectual issues concerning what kind of a character I was thereby constructing for Hannah and with what kind of consequence for my relationship with and understanding of her, as well as the consequences for how both Hannah's diaries and her relationship with Munby would be read and understood.

While editing the Cullwick diaries for publication, as I noted at the beginning of this chapter, I was asked to write an essay on Olive Schreiner. In doing so I became interested in the role of Olive Schreiner's estranged husband, Samuel "Cron" Cronwright-Schreiner (he took her name on marriage), in establishing a particular characterization of Schreiner through his widower's biography of her (Cronwright-Schreiner, 1924a) and his edited (to the extent of sometimes fabrication and sometimes eradication) collection of her letters (Cronwright-Schreiner 1924b). Because of the apparent paucity of other sources, his view has formed an important pivot of a feminist biography of Schreiner (Ruth First & Ann Scott, 1980), which has utilized his highly motivated, syrupy, yet ruthlessly negative, construction of her in the biography known to Olive Schreiner's friends as "Cronwright's novel."

My initial aim was to provide an alternative reading of the life and work of Olive Schreiner (Stanley, 1983) to that contained in Ruth First and Ann Scott's, in my view, problematic treatment. Later, through textual analytic means, I examined in detail the Cronwright-Schreiner biography as an exemplar of the "ideological three-step" identified by Dorothy Smith (1974) in using Marx and Engels' (1968) views on how to unpick and analyze material ideological practices (Stanley, 1986b). I began to focus on how readers engage with the structure as well as the content of a particular piece of writing. Cronwright-Schreiner had stripped from small snippets of Schreiner's behavior and highlights of her character the contextual specifics (which can be pieced back together from other sources) that established these as reasonable responses to particular occasions and moments; in great contrast he presents them as instead generalized and context-transferable permanent traits indicative of the "inner" and "real" character of Olive Schreiner. This character or personality is of an irredeemably flawed genius, "difficult" and indeed apparently almost impossible to engage with at an interpersonal level.

Biographies, or at least the form that they conventionally take, are oddities. In Victoria Glendinning's (1983) phrase, they place under the spotlight one individual alone, casting everyone else into the shadows. This is singularly unlike life, where the lives of even the famous and infamous are densely populated by peers. Only on paper does one person alone occupy a stage and the limelight. And only on paper is that limelighted person seen through the views of one commentator alone, one singular commentator who selects the evidence presented, decides what to include and exclude, which of the friends and lovers and enemies and acquaintances are significant and which not, what is meaningful and what trivial.

Cronwright-Schreiner was a very singular commentator, who took a good deal of trouble to permit only one sharply clear Olive to enter his pages. The Olive Schreiner that other people experienced as changeable, magnetic, fun, bewildering, and infuriating; unanswerable in the clarity of her views and unshakable in her feminism, pacifism, and socialism; surrounded by dearly loved and loving feminist friends, nowhere gets a look in. The textual means he utilized are observable enough to readers who suspend trust and do not simply accept the biographer's goodwill, trumpeted though it is. However, Cronwright-Schreiner's method is not in essentials different from the typical and acceptable means of any biographer. What distinguishes him is his lack of goodwill and his supplementary activity in changing and modifying the content of original documents, such as letters. Otherwise the textual means he utilized are standard, legitimate practices in producing a life of any biographical subject. Of course autobiographers can be as complicit as biographers, indeed typically more so, in producing a life as a seamless whole in which there is seemingly a clear linear development from beginning to if not an end, then at least a plateau. But lives are like this only in the retelling; living them the first time around, before they and their events are retold by us or by others, is a much messier business.

Olive Schreiner, in other contemporaries' views of her, lived deeply embedded in overlapping networks of feminist friendship. It is rare to read contemporary British reminiscences—diaries, letters—of feminists and of radical and literary people and not find Olive Schreiner enter in a whirl of activity at some point. Thus another trajectory of interest, also engendered by my earlier Olive Schreiner essay, became centered on feminist social networks or "webs of friendship" (Liz Stanley, 1986a).

I chose six British feminist women that Olive Schreiner met and became friendly with to a lesser or greater degree—Eleanor Marx, Emma Cons, Edith Lees, Constance Lytton, Dora Montefiore, and Virginia Woolf—and traced each of their feminist involvements and connections. In doing so, I compared the divisions of formal feminist organizations with the complexities of interconnections between feminist women who, in their interpersonal involvements, often healed such divisions by being actively involved with each other across formal lines of separation.

The work I did here was temporally "flat," excluding the dimension of time and the changes it brings to the nature of friendship. That is, although the period I covered in looking at these friendship patterns was from approximately 1800 to 1939, each friendship was included as simply itself, rather than a tracing of its beginnings, developments, and sometimes endings. To confess its ahistorical cast is not to deny this work's meaning and purpose, however, for my intention was a simple one: to investigate whether, using existing published sources based on the "spotlight" approach, such interconnections were recoverable. Succinctly, I thought that feminist women of the past, like those of the present, were likely to have known and engaged with each other on informal interpersonal levels as well as formal organizational ones; I wanted to know whether what was already published would tell me if this was so; and, if it could, I wanted to know who knew whom. My concern was thus with an extremely unromantic notion of feminist friendship, as being connected, rather than being committed. As I said at the outset of this chapter, respect seems to me more important than liking or loving, for people can and often do base close dealings with each other on factors other than these emotions.

FEMINIST BIOGRAPHICAL METHOD

What I have just outlined in connection with some of the biographical work I have carried out are the elements involved in my construction of a feminist biographical method. I have arrived at the understanding descriptively glossed in the previous section piecemeal, and of course not only out of my biographical practices but also other factors within my autobiography: deaths of some of those close to me, movements away of friends, new relationships, neighbors, colleagues, books read, events in the world political situation, television programs, and much much more that cannot even be glossed. All this is specific to me; and the understanding or knowledge I have outlined above is very much located in and predicated upon process within my life: a very material process in which these ideas have been produced. This process is specific to me indeed; however, little of it is unique to me, for very similar understandings have been pieced together by other feminists working out of different traditions and with very different lives. Ideas are common property and a product of their time, not of individual thinkers.

In summary the elements of feminist biographic method as I understand it are:

1. an a priori insistence that works of biography should be treated as composed by textually located ideological practices—of course including any biography produced by the feminist biographer herself—and analytically engaged with as such;
2. a textual recognition of the importance of the labor process of the biographer as researcher in reaching the interpretations and conclusions she does: what I would call "intellectual autobiography" (Stanley, 1984b), that is, an analytic (not just descriptive) concern with the specifics of how we come to understand what we do, by locating acts of understanding in an explication of the grounded contexts these are located in and arise from;
3. a rejection of the spotlight approach to a single individual, but also and relatedly a recognition that the informal organization of feminists through friendship can be as important as formal feminist organization in understanding the dynamics and complexities of such women's lives.

For me these are the key elements of method and of form for producing feminist biography in ways influenced by feminist epistemology and feminist sociology (see Stanley, 1990a on method in feminist sociology; Stanley & Wise, 1990 for a discussion of debates concerning feminist epistemology). Each element was important in the work I did with Ann Morley (1988) looking at the role of Emily Wilding Davison and her "militant" friends in the Women's Social and Political Union (WSPU), the so-called "suffragettes." This book was written as, among other things, an account of the labor process involved in producing it. It contains both the first feminist biography of Emily Davison and the history of how and why this came to be written, and written by the person it was. It also provides commentary on the various histories of the Edwardian feminist movement and the ways in which these treat the WSPU as a deviant mainstream political organization rather than evaluating it through the myriad of feminist informal activities and involvements that coexisted within and alongside the formal organization.

In tracing out the patterns of comradeship of Emily Davison and her closest colleagues, a rather different view is established of the WSPU and its dealings with other contemporary feminist organizations than is found in even feminist histories. Our research suggested very strongly that friendship (in both senses referred to earlier) is a surer guide to feminist practical political realities that the machinations of and divisions between national (usually London-based and oriented) formal feminist organizations and their dealings with mainstream and very malestream parliamentary politics. In particular, we show that the development of and changes in "militancy" can be adequately explained only by reference to internal feminist political factors, not as a tactic in relation to parliamentary politics. And not as the invention of Christabel Pankhurst either, but rather the determined product of opposition to leadership betrayals and failures by the most radical WSPU women, a product then adopted and widely used in often very different ways by others.

As I emphasized earlier, ideas are neither individually produced nor individually owned, but common products of shared experiences and of their places and times. More than this, implicit so far but needing to be made explicit, is the conviction that ideas are products of a *material* labor process. The conventional materialist feminist view that ideology and materiality are separate and the former is different in kind from the latter is one I cannot accept. It seems to me a decidely unmaterialist thing to argue; moreover, it removes from analytical sight all that is interesting about ideology, as a set of material and analyzable activities, and the analytic method for investigating ideological practices first developed by Marx and Engels. I stress this here because, relatedly, I am arguing that due analytic attention should be given by feminists to the labor process wherein ideas about a biographical subject are located and materially produced. I want feminism to recover ideology, not as the false practices of "baddies" but rather the material production of ideas by everyone, including "goodies" such as feminists.

It has become conventional to depict a concern with lives as a concern with decorticated individuals, in which there is a focus on their uniqueness, greatness, and specialness: biography as a concern with famous dead men and feminist biography as a concern with famous (but not as famous) dead women. It is certainly true that the dominant convention in biography production is to work, indeed to think, in such terms; this is encouraged by conventional ideas about literary production, which see the genesis of a text outside of both the piece of writing itself and the social and temporal conditions within which it is located, and inside the writer as a special and different kind of person. However, there is no necessity for such a limited view of biography and there is every reason why feminist biographers in particular should reject such rampant individualism.

This conviction is one shared with a good many other feminists, who have similarly sought to use biography to look at interconnections between particular groups of women. For instance, Gillian Hanscombe and Virginia Smyers (1987) looked at a network of women writers influenced by modernism; Barbara Caine (1986) at the lives, work and feminism of the Potter sisters; and Philippa Levine (1990) at networks of friendship and political interconnection between feminist women from the 1850s to 1900.

It is also often argued that a concern with an auto/biographical self necessarily trades on essentialist and/or reductionist ideas about a "real self." It is certainly true that one of the main forms autobiographies have taken is tracing out the unfettering of a real inner self (as, for example, in feminist factional form in Marilyn French's [1977] *The Women's Room*); more recently Freudian and Lacanian ideas about the self have greatly influenced people who write about autobiography (see Shari Benstock, 1988; Donna Stanton, 1987; compare with Dale Spender, 1987, which works out of a different and less reductionist idea of the self). However, this is by no means necessary emphasis, and equally illustrious alternative constructions of self can be found.

Virginia Woolf (1976), for example, uses the notion of "moments of being" to describe those apparently crystal-clear collections of memories that are rafts that link our past and present self. This is a social, not psychological, understanding of self as both ontologically fragile and continually renewed by self-conscious acts of memory and writing. Rosemary Manning (1971) has written an apparently conventional autobiography but which is, in fact; the record and proof of how, after an almost successful suicide attempt, she goes about the business of constructing a different self, a self who is capable of living. She then (1987) uses a "corridor of mirrors" metaphor to describe the assemblage of selves that we present in life, and also to suggest the artfulness of autobiography in constructing an apparently factual self for public showing. Typically, biographers are much less ready to deal openly with such complexities in the nature of the self. But again there are exceptions to be found, as when Gertrude Stein (1933) wrote what is apparently a biography of her lover Alice Toklas, but is actually an autobiography of herself; and later (1938), she wrote what is apparently an autobiography but is actually a biography of the human social condition, *Everybody's Autobiography*.

Also on the unallowable individualism theme, to suggest that feminist biography should be reflexively concerned with its own production—with its own labor process—has been interpreted as mere narcissism. That is, it is seen as a narrow and limited focus on the biographer herself, as well as on her subject. I find it truly paradoxical that a concern with process—with opening up biographical and other feminist research processes for scrutiny by readers—should be so labeled, particularly when such a charge emanates from other feminist social scientists. Lurking behind such a criticism is in fact a slip into psychological reductionist thinking: If you aren't writing about people en masse then what you're doing is neither social nor sociological. I would rebut this with the last breath in my feminist sociologist's body: I stand four-square by the conviction—fundamental to sociology—that people are social beings through and through, and that social structures are as recoverable from single social beings as they are from groups of them (see Sally Cline, 1984, for a telling demonstration of this in terms of the power of the word "lesbian" in structuring one woman's presented and articulated identity).

There are additional good feminist reasons for rejecting this criticism. The aim and consequence of the approach I have outlined is to enable more people than just one—the biographer—to analytically engage with the biographical investigative or research process. For instance, Carolyn Steedman's (1986) *Landscape for a Good Woman* points out the severe limitations of most feminist work for those of us who are not middle class (and I would also add, not white or heterosexual) and emphasizes how interwoven her own autobiography is with her construction of her mother's biography; it also illuminatingly shows the reader that understanding these links involves a process within which her changing thinking was located. Similarly Kim Chernin's (1985) *In My Mother's House: A Daughter's Story* does not simply invoke her changing comprehension of her mother's life and so her own: she shows this by locating it within richly detailed episodes and stories. It is difficult—I find it impossible—to see how the epithets "narcissistic" or "limited" can be applied to work such as this, which I find immensely open, concerned to reject a narrow version of self and to argue instead for its social construction within a network of others, and determined to make apparent differences between women rather than glossing their similarities through generalizations about groups.

PROCESS IN FEMINIST EPISTEMOLOGY

Discussions of feminist epistemology (Sandra Harding, 1987; Dorothy Smith, 1987; Liz Stanley, 1990b) and of ideas concerning feminist auto/biography are two particularly fruitful areas of current academic feminist debate and writing. Although both are preoccupied with the same fundamental questions—what "feminism" should look like in life but also in textual terms, what should be the proper relationship between feminist researchers and the "subjects" of their research, what should be the relationship between experience and feminist theory—these discussions have been conducted in parallel. Issues concerning the researcher's self have only hesitantly been considered in discussions of feminist research; while epistemological issues concerning feminist research in general have been considered only in passing in relation to the specifics of feminist auto/biography. There is much to be gained by bringing these two important debates closer together. I briefly sketch, around the notion of analytically engaging with the idea and actuality of process, one site for doing so.

There has been resistance on the part of many feminist social science academics to become concerned with experience—both that of research subjects and that of researchers themselves. Experience, it is claimed, is a kind of pretheoretical morass; feminist analysis necessarily transcends this by injecting theory into it or perhaps drawing theory out of it, depending on the analogy being used. Similarly, a focus on process in research terms is deemed necessarily a- or even antitheoretical: as experience is termed pretheoretical, so too is process in social life (and including, it would seem, in research). The kind of simple dichotomous model which underpins such a view can be depicted figuratively (as in Figure 1). Here academics, and academic feminists among them, are construed as the producers of knowledge, the constructors and guardians of epistemology; the process engaged in to produce knowledge is seen as science and so, by definition, analytical; the structure of analysis is seen as necessarily logical. Experience or being, in sharp contrast, is seen as characterized by its production of stories or accounts; these are defined as descriptive and not analytic; its description is seen as essentially narratively structured story-telling rather than logically structured argument. The corollary of such a dichotomous model is to locate academic feminists among the scientists, and the rest of humanity among those who merely experience but do not analyze or theorize and certainly do not construct epistemological frames of reference and use.

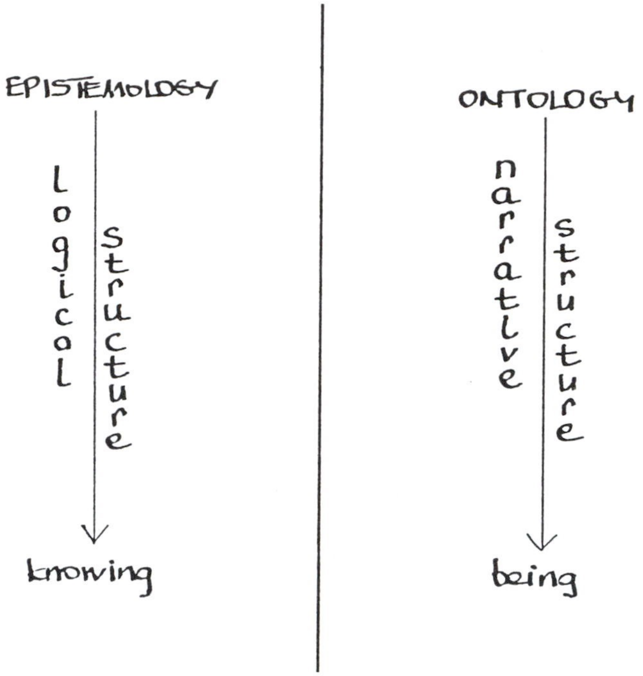

FIGURE 1. The "science" model of knowing and being

I find this model, and its accompanying academic practices, depressingly antifeminist and I reject its crude "Scientistic" (Jürgen Habermas, 1972) assumptions. As an account of the production of feminist ideas, moreover, it is just plain wrong. The most exciting feminist rethinking (see Susan Brownmiller, 1975; Shulamith Firestone, 1972; Germaine Greer, 1970; Kate Millet, 1971; Juliet Mitchell, 1971; Sheila Rowbotham, 1973), those ideas which have now influenced millions of women, have been produced out of a process which takes narrative of women's lives and views; a post hoc account structured by process, seriously at an analytic and theory-producing level. The production of feminist ideas can be presented figuratively as in Figure 2: a model of knowledge production which rejects a dichotomized relationship between epistemology and ontology, seeing these as rather symbiotically related.

So what has this to do with feminist biography? A biography, typically, is a chronological narrative which tells the story of a life. Its defining concern is with being, with the nature of ontological existence as seen within the exemplar of the life investigated and discussed. At its most basic, then, biography lies firmly on the side (in terms of the Scientistic model) of experience rather than analysis, ontology rather than epistemology. However—

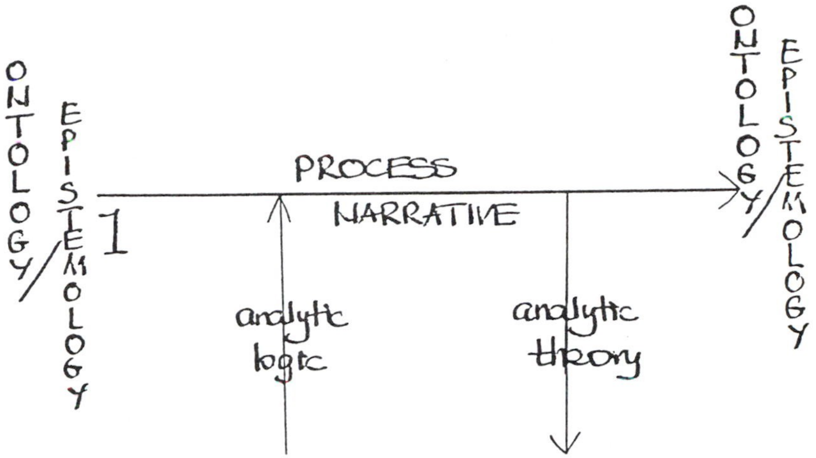

FIGURE 2. A feminist model of knowing and being

and it is a most significant however—biography is not only a narrative; it is also and equally self-evidently based on *investigation,* on *inquiry,* and on a process of selection in and out of not only the facts but the *salient* facts. It is, to express it in the rhetoric of epistemology, a theory: a theory of a character or a person, but a theory nonetheless.

A serious discussion of the processes by which biography is produced makes available to us telling evidence of how the supposed dichotomies of epistemology and ontology are breached, indeed sealed, by producing analysis out of narrative. Similarly so, a serious analytic attention to (feminist and all other) academic research processes makes available a converse breaching and sealing of conventional dichotomies: an analytically engaged-with account of the process by which knowledge is produced out of research practices puts the narrative, the chronology, and the contextual specifics that underpin all knowledges back into epistemology.

A BRIEF SUMMING UP

A conclusion would be a most unfitting way to finish a chapter concerned with process. In addition, I have been arguing about beginnings, developments, and changes; conclusions are neither possible nor desirable, for they would foreclose what should be an ongoing and lively debate. So I finish by summing up what I see as the main trajectories of my argument.

As I have tried to show, my own working practices as a biographer have changed a good deal, and increasingly in the direction of recognizing within the written work I produce the contextually specific material factors that initiate thoughts, lines of investigation, and conclusions. The process of producing biography is as interesting and certainly as exciting as its product;

more than this, to account for the product—by taking seriously at an analytical level the labor process that produces it—enables a much more active engagement by the reader with what is published and read/consumed.

Ideas, I have argued, may take specific forms in particular people's lives; but ideas are more properly to be seen as the product and property of their times, of materially located and behaving sets of people. I have said this in relation to my own ideas about a feminist biographic method, noting that other feminists interested in biography have developed similar working and writing practices as I. One of those shared working practices is an awareness of this common production of ideas in relation to biographic subjects. Instead of the spotlight approach, focusing on one single person, many feminist biographers (and indeed autobiographers such as Chernin, 1985; Steedman, 1986) are rather concerned with groups and collectivities of women: Women acting in concert with or opposition to each other. Such a development seems to me one of the most interesting and exciting directions *all* biographical writing could move in.

There are reasons for feminists to give attention to investigative processes in addition to the greater empowerment of readers. Feminist analysis of the late 1960s and early 1970s was predicated on an awareness of the baleful contribution of dichotomized understandings of the nature and meaning of social life to women's oppression: the dichotomies theory versus practice, objective versus subjective, and reason versus emotion, were among them. I find it ironic that some academic feminists are now in the business of reinventing such dichotomies, but positioning themselves on a different side of the divide from the mass of women (and indeed from the mass of men). One of these reinvented and newly respectable dichotomies is that between experience and analysis, with the role of academic feminists being marked out as the analyzers and theorizers of other women's experiences.

What a close analytic attention to the processes by which science and knowledge are produced reveals, however, is that experience and analysis are actually very much the same thing. All analysis, both lay and professional, is grounded in a material context in which is located not only behavior in the narrow sense, but also conjecture, thought, investigation, discussion, conclusion, and the retelling of all these in narrative form. Science looks different because the rhetoric through which it is expressed systematically denies the role of chronology and narrative; instead it is structured through a form which takes analysis out of the time and place it was a product of, and into a more formal logical framework in which ideas are related to each other rather than the material conditions which give rise to them.

Biography, or at least a biographic form that deals with collectivities and is expressed in terms of process, shows clearly that any posited dichotomy between epistemology and ontology, between knowing and being, or between analysis and experience, is a false dichotomy and should be rejected along with the other apparatus of Scientism. Feminist biography as I conceive it would adopt such a form, and thus become analytically and theoretically, concerned with method.

Biographies are as popular as they are because they tell an interesting story and usually tell it accessibly and enjoyably; because they apparently let us into lives different from our own; and because they can provide feminist heroes to stand alongside the more usual subjects of biography. These sources of interest need to be recognized and accepted as entirely legitimate ones in feminist terms, not treated as supposedly naive. Nonetheless, we still need to develop the means for a more active engagement by the reader with biographical writing—one that does not take this on trust as a source of indisputable fact but rather recognizes its role in the construction of particular views of the self it presents.

Just as important as the question of how feminists should *read* biographies is the question of whether and in what ways there could be distinct feminist ways of *writing* them. I have argued that such means exist and are located in an analytic attention to method and to process as well as to the positioning of biographic subjects in the social and political circles that were important to them and in which their individual lives have meaning.

REFERENCES

Barthes, Roland. (1980). *Camera lucida*. London: Flamingo.

Benstock, Shari (Ed.). (1988). *The private self: Theory and practice of women's autobiographical writings*. London: Routledge

Berger, John. (1972). *Ways of seeing*. Harmondsworth: Penguin.

Brownmiller, Susan. (1975). *Against our will*. London: Secker & Warburg.

Caine, Barbara. (1986). *Destined to be wives: The sisters of Beatrice Webb*. Oxford: Clarendon Press.

Chernin, Kim. (1985). *In my mother's house: A daughter's story*. London: Virago Press.

Cline, Sally. (1984). The case of Beatrice: An analysis of the word "lesbian" and the power of language to control women. In Olivia Butler (Ed.), *Feminist experience in feminist research* (pp. 5–32). Studies in Sexual Politics no.2, Sociology Department, University of Manchester.

Cronwright-Schreiner, Samuel. (1924a). *The life of Olive Schreiner*. New York: Haskell House.

Cronwright-Schreiner, Samuel (Ed.). (1924b). *The letters of Olive Schreiner*. London: Fisher Unwin.

Firestone, Shulamith. (1972). *The dialectic of sex*. London: Paladin.

First, Ruth, & Scott, Ann. (1980). *Olive Schreiner*. London: The Women's Press.

French, Marilyn. (1977). *The women's room*. London: Sphere.

Glendinning, Victoria. (1983). *Vita: Life of Vita Sackville-West* Harmondsworth: Penguin.

Goffman, Erving. (1976). *Gender advertisements*. London: Macmillan.

Greer, Germaine. (1970). *The female eunuch*. London: Paladin.

Habermas, Jürgen. (1972). *Knowledge and human interest*. London: Heinemann.

Hanscombe, Gillian, & Smyers, Virginia. (1987). *Writing for their lives: The modernist women 1910–1940*. London: The Women's Press.
Harding, Sandra (Ed.). (1987). *Feminism and methodology*. Milton Keynes: Open Univerity Press.
Hudson, Derek (Ed.). (1972). *Munby: Man of two worlds*. London: John Murray.
Levine, Philippa. (1990). Love, friendship and feminism in later nineteenth century England. *Women's Studies International Forum, 13*(1/2) 63–78.
Manning, Rosemary. (1971). *A time and a time*. London: Marion Boyars. (Originally published under the pseudonym of Sarah Davys)
Manning, Rosemary. (1987). *A corridor of mirrors*. London: The Women's Press.
Marx, Karl, & Engels, Frederick. (1968). *The german ideology*. Moscow: Progress.
Millett, Kate. (1971). *Sexual politics*. London: Abacus.
Mitchell, Juliet. (1971). *Woman's estate*. Harmondsworth: Penguin.
Rowbotham, Sheila. (1973). *Woman's consciousness, man's world*. Harmondsworth: Penguin.
Smith, Dorothy. (1974). Theorising as ideology. In Roy Turner (Ed.), *Ethnomethodology* (pp. 41–44). Harmondsworth: Penguin.
Smith, Dorothy. (1987). *The everyday world as problematic: A feminist sociology*. Milton Keynes: Open University Press.
Sontag, Susan. (1978). *On photography*. Harmondsworth: Penguin.
Spence, Jo. (1986). *Putting myself in the picture: A political personal and photographic autobiography*. London: Camden Press.
Spender, Dale (Ed.). (1983). *Feminist theorists*. London: The Women's Press.
Spender, Dale (Ed.). (1987). Personal chronicles: Women's autobiographical writings [Special issue]. *Women's Studies International Forum, 10*(1).
Stanley, Liz. (1983). Olive Schreiner: New women, free women, all women. In Dale Spender (Ed.), *Feminist theorists* (pp. 229–243). London: The Women's Press.
Stanley, Liz (Ed.). (1984a). *The Diaries of Hannah Cullwick*. London: Virago Press.
Stanley, Liz. (1984b). How the social science research process discriminates against women. in Sandra Acker & David Warren-Piper (Eds.), *Is higher education fair to women?* (pp. 189–209). London: Nelson.
Stanley, Liz. (1986a). Feminism and friendship in England from 1825 to 1938. in *Feminism and friendship: Two essays on Olive Schreiner* (pp. 10–46) Studies in Sexual Politics no.8, University of Manchester.
Stanley, Liz. (1986b). How Olive Schreiner vanished, leaving behind only her asthmatic personality. In *Feminism and Friendship. Two Essays on Olive Schreiner* (pp. 47–79). Studies in Sexual Politics no.8, University of Manchester.
Stanley, Liz. (1987a). Biography as microscope or kaleidoscope? The case of "power" in Hannah Cullwick's relationship with Arthur Munby. *Women's Studies International Forum, 10*(1), 19–31.
Stanley, Liz. (1987b). Editing Hannah Cullwick's diaries. In Feminist Research Seminar (Eds.), *Feminist research processes* (pp. 88–89). Studies in Sexual Politics no.16, Sociology Department, University of Manchester.
Stanley, Liz, with Morley, Ann. (1988). *The life and death of Emily Wilding Davison*. London: The Women's Press.
Stanley, Liz (Ed.). (1990a). *Feminist praxis: Research, theory and epistemology in feminist sociology*. London: Routledge.
Stanley, Liz. (1990b,). Ordinary phallacies: A textual analysis of an interview with D. M. Thomas. In Liz Stanley (Ed.), *Feminist praxis: Research, theory and epistemology in feminist sociology*. London: Routledge.
Stanley, Liz. (in press). *The auto/biographical I: Theory and practice of feminist auto/biography*. Manchester: Manchester University Press.
Stanley, Liz, & Wise, Sue. (1990) Method, methodology and epistemology in femi-

nist research processes. In Liz Stanley (Ed.), *Feminist praxis: Research, theory and epistemology in feminist sociology*. London: Routledge.

Stanton, Domna (Ed.). (1987). *The female autograph*. Chicago: University of Chicago Press.

Steedman, Carolyn. (1986). *Landscape for a good woman*. London: Virago Press.

Stein, Gertrude. (1933). *The autobiography of Alice B. Toklas*. Harmondsworth: Penguin.

Stein, Gertrude. (1938). *Everybody's autobiography*. London: Virago Press.

Swindells, Julia. (1986, May). Liberating the subject? Autobiography and "women's history:" A reading of *The Diaries of Hannah Cullwick*. University of Minnesota Center for Advanced Feminist Studies Conference on "Autobiographies, Biographies and Life Histories of Women: Interdisciplinary Perspectives." University of Minnesota, Minneapolis.

Woolf, Virginia. (1976). *Moments of being*. London: Chatto & Windus.

Chapter 12
Woman to Woman

Margaret Forster

On June 29th, 1984, I visited the Casa Guidi in Florence knowing very little about the famous poets who had lived there a hundred or more years ago. Like most people, I had a confused and highly romanticized vision of Elizabeth Barrett Browning, compiled mainly from memories of film versions of *The Barretts of Wimpole Street* (1930), in which she was presented as a frail and terrified invalid finally released from her father's tyrannical power by Robert Browning. But stuck somewhere in my head I also had a vague impression that the woman who had written *Aurora Leigh* could not be quite so frail and also that there was some suggestion of contradiction between legend and work. I went to the Casa Guidi out of simple curiosity and of course it was the strengthening, rather than the satisfying, of this curiosity which finally led me to want to write Elizabeth Barrett Browning's biography.

What I was curious about was the woman more than the work—at least at first. The Casa Guidi is an eerie place, even on a blindingly hot summer day. You enter into a dark and dismal hallway and climb stone steps to the first floor where the Brownings had their apartment, and which is now half shrine, half museum. Nothing is as I had imagined: The rooms are vast and gloomy; the famous balcony, from which Elizabeth watched so many processions, a mere strip of an affair; all views from the rooms are blocked by the side of the San Felice church. It feels unwelcoming and sinister. With the thought in my head that this was more spooky than Wimpole Street and half as attractive, I went into the bedroom where Elizabeth gave birth to her son and where she died—the feeling of claustrophobia, although the rooms are so big, increased. Then the curator took out of a drawer a christening robe, saying it was Pen's, Elizabeth's son's. I held it, pristine in its newly cleaned and restored state, and suddenly I found myself trying to focus on a poet who was a wife, a lover, and a mother as well as a legend. What about her life *after* Wimpole Street? What about her domestic set up? What about how her duties as wife and mother affected her work? What, in short, about Elizabeth Barrett Browning as a woman?

To begin at the beginning was made absurdly easy thanks to the publication of the *Browning Correspondence*. (Kelley & Hudson, 1984a, 1984b, 1985, 1986, 1987, 1988, 1989). By a wonderful coincidence volume one, full of new letters dating from 1809 (when Elizabeth was only three years old) was published in 1984, so I went straight into intimate glimpses of Elizabeth as a child and adolescent. At once, her gender leapt out as of enormous importance. There it all is—her furious jealousy at her brothers' better chances of formal education, her rage at having to sew and sketch and tinkle on the piano when they went off hunting and shooting and generally careering around at liberty. Every woman remembers the moment, even in these strongly and thankfully feminist times, when she comes up against the limitations imposed on her by her sex. The cry "it's not *fair*" echoes throughout Elizabeth's early correspondence, and of course in the early 19th century things not being fair were a great deal more serious. Nobody has ever had the chance before to go into how rebellious Elizabeth was and to see her revolt against being a woman. Up to now, she's been presented to us, near the age of 40, as the most submissive person in the world, apparently hardly knowing a pang of discontent. But in the very first volume of this correspondence it is painfully obvious she had had to learn submission.

I found watching her learn submission sometimes unbearably poignant. She could not believe her fate, or what seemed certain to be her fate, and I watched her make the same calculations and come to the same crude and naive conclusions as I came to myself in such different times. Male biographers (not one of whom likes Elizabeth anyway, seeing her as an episode in Robert's life and a drag at that) have been unable to understand Elizabeth's antisocial tendencies and her avowed attitude to marriage when she was still a young and attractive woman. They write of her as petulant, perhaps even double-bluffing as a cover for not receiving any proposals, whereas she was in a state of panic and shock as she grew up and saw what marriage was. She looked around and saw what happened when a woman married: She lost her individuality and was smothered in children who drained her of all vitality. Very well! If marriage equalled surrender of oneself then it was very simple: Do not marry. If love tricked you into marriage then it was also simple: Do not allow yourself to love. Men were traps to be avoided and if your nature and your body craved what they offered, be stern and stifle such stirrings or all would be lost.

There is nothing funny about this, nor is it trivial. All art starts somewhere and Elizabeth Barrett Browning's started in this kicking against being a woman, with all that meant. For almost a decade—from the age of 14, when her highly imitative *Battle of Marathon* (1820) was published, to the age of 22, when the death of her mother changed the direction of her poetry—Elizabeth's feminist tendencies were well hidden. She was so depressed at the kind of life she was compelled to lead as a woman that she could do no more than try to think of higher things, which led her poetry into deeply religious grooves. Her father approved of this and because his approval mattered at that stage it was a factor in her art. But beneath the convincing facade of resignation the spirit of rebellion was very much there. Elizabeth *tried* to assure herself and everyone else that all she wanted to do was stay at home with her loving family and write poetry about religious feelings and grief and sorrow but she could not help dreaming of another life. What she most wanted in that dream life was not just to travel but to associate with "like minds." These would be "true poets," like herself, and inevitably they would be men because she could only think of two contemporary female poets worthy of the name. She struggled, as women still struggle today, to assure herself that having what people called "a masculine mind" was nonsense, but she failed. She did actually believe that her mind was of such sharpness that it was masculine, and that she ought to be proud and not ashamed of acknowledging this. What encouraged her in this belief was the mediocre mental caliber of the women who surrounded her. Her mother was clever and educated but nevertheless was not given to quite the academic turn of mind Elizabeth admired, nor did she relish intellectual argument; her two sisters were not in the least interested in any kind of intellectual activity; her Aunt Bummy, who often stayed with the Barretts and acted as a stand-in for their mother when she died, was very much on a par with most matrons of the day in positively disapproving of too much writing and reading; and the majority of the women neighbors in Herefordshire, where the Barretts lived at the time, were more interested in dinners and balls.

So Elizabeth dreamed of escaping and finding other poets who would overlook her womanly shape and accept her for her "masculine" mind. She wanted her femaleness set aside so she could be seen for what she was—a powerful intellect inside a girlish frame. Her discontent with her situation rises like a vapor from the pages of a diary she kept between June 1831 and April 1832. No woman could be fooled by it. Men have scented only a disgruntled girl desperately hoping for more than she is ever going to get, because the diary is mainly a record of Elizabeth's relationship with a blind, Greek scholar who had come to live near her and had offered his friendship (intellectual of course). The scholar, Hugh Stuart Boyd, was a married, middle-aged man with a daughter almost Elizabeth's own age. He liked Elizabeth to read Greek to him and she was only too eager, believing him to be the friend she had needed for so long. But Boyd in the end not only caused her intense distress by his emotional rejection of her but also forced her to face up to her own nature. There was no question of any love affair with Boyd in our understanding of the phrase and neither Boyd nor Elizabeth ever thought there was, but at the same time there was a strong undercurrent of passion in Elizabeth's expectations of Boyd which she found difficulty in controlling. Boyd, she concluded, was cold and "coldness, coldness, coldness is what I cannot bear." She was, she told her diary, like an iron which "hisses" when it is spat on. What she wanted from people was warmth and intimacy. What Boyd offered was a sterile, formal friendship and she hated it.

The realization that she looked for more and had more—much more—to offer, radically changed Elizabeth's assessment of her own nature. She was, after all, a woman and being a woman seemed to mean that no matter how hard she tried to be satisfied with intellectual pursuits she was not; half herself was stifled. It is no coincidence that in the year after her mother died, which was the second year of her friendship with Boyd, Elizabeth's poetry began to change. Creeping into it came the theme of why *should* women surrender their true natures to men? Why could they not be hearts as well as minds and bodies as well as intellects? Side by side was the growing suspicion of a contempt for men who did not realize what they spurned and took advantage of their own willful ignorance. But recognizing the reality of her passionate nature, acknowledging that it was there and would not go away however hard she studied and absorbed herself in work did not at that stage help Elizabeth. It made her even more miserable. She felt, in her late 20s, that she was coming to a crisis. The only place for her passion to go was into her poetry, and even there it had to be heavily disguised. She wrote what the public thought were sweet and charming ballads, but which were, in fact, vicious attacks on prevailing standards of courtship, and lyrics which read as light and amusing but which were sharp and incisive underneath.

Meanwhile, the dreary road to the Wimpole Street couch we all know so well stretched out before her. By the time she was 38, and about to publish a two-volume edition of the poems that made her name, Elizabeth Barrett really did think she had given up all thoughts of ever finding any outlet other than her poetry for her "womanly nature." Like most women of that age, now as then, she had to convince herself she had made the better bargain than all those downtrodden, betrayed wives she saw around her, asking scornfully, "where *are* the happy marriages?" She was, she told herself and her friend Mary Russell Mitford, past such things as love and marriage and not sorry to be. But then I read her letters to Miss Mitford about the French novels they both loved, especially those of George Sand, and especially *Leila*. Elizabeth's excitement at the sexual and sensual descriptions in that novel is manifest—she said *Leila* was a "soul-slime" of a book and that she ought to have dropped it into the fire (but didn't). She wrote quite breathlessly to Miss Mitford of the power of that novel, and it is easy to calculate the even deeper inner effect it had on her. The trouble was that it made her aware of what she had *not* experienced, which was agony—a whole life experience she had missed and could never now know. It led her to ask herself if any woman could ever be said to have fulfilled herself if she had never had a chance to explore this side of herself.

Robert Browning appeared on the scene and gave Elizabeth that chance. Although she dictated that this should be a platonic relationship and nothing more she was never fooled about her response to him. She was instead terrified. The violence of her reaction to Robert's presence took her completely by surprise, and the minute she realized its strength she began to panic because she could not believe he felt the same way about her. How could he, she tortured herself, when she was plain (she was not), emaciated through illness, and old? Giving Elizabeth confidence in herself *as a woman* was the hardest task Robert Browning ever had. She was impossible to compliment. Tell her she was beautiful and she assumed she was being mocked; say she was the most wonderful woman in the world, such as he had never met before, and she almost wept with humiliation; swear you were dizzy with love for her and would not be able to answer for your action if she greeted you standing up and she was mortified. When Elizabeth wrote *Sonnets from the Portuguese* during this courtship she poured out all her own insecurity as a woman. Again and again she repeats in sonnet after sonnet what a poor, unworthy, unattractive person she is, not worthy of any man's notice. Her final admission that her love was truly reciprocated was "the wonder of her life."

It is painful to discover how literary London sniggered over the Brownings' marriage and flight. As Elizabeth had predicted, the world judged them both "mad and bad." An invalid spinster of 40 running off with a penniless poet 6 years younger? It was indecent. The assumption was made that sex could not come into it (although the Victorians expressed themselves differently and much more crudely). When Elizabeth gave birth 21/2 years later to her son, it was obvious they had been wrong—this was a "proper" marriage. It was not only proper but supremely passionate. Elizabeth no longer needed to read *Leila* and yearn. To her sister Arabel she wrote with unmistakable emphasis that Robert was perfect "in every way" and her descriptions of him being "far too tender with me" plus her line that being with him "is like riding an enchanted horse" leave very little to the imagination. She was sexually fulfilled and after the birth of her son had also answered what she referred to as "the supreme calling" in becoming a mother.

Theoretically, what should have followed was a waning of her poetical powers and it is true that the desire to write was for a while absent. This has puzzled male biographers unnecessarily and some have used it to suggest Elizabeth was always just sublimating her instincts in poetry until such time as a man came along. A monstrous allegation, often flung at women, and hardly necessary to refute. But it is undeniable that when Elizabeth did start writing again—after only what was a relatively short interval—she had changed. Being a wife and mother had made a difference but not in the way people expected. It had made her tougher, more determined to use her poetry to fight causes; the happier she was with Robert, the more she grieved for women less fortunate than herself; the more convinced she became of Robert's goodness, the surer she was of the average man's wickedness. Her sense of responsibility, for the evils women were exposed to, grew daily. It was, she felt, up to her and others equally lucky to tell the world what went on and to change it: hence *Aurora Leigh*.

Elizabeth said she had no sympathy with "these woman's rights people" which has led biographers ever since to label her, on her own admission, as antifeminist. She was not. Like her detractors, she misunderstood the nature of feminism, which has very little to do with the kind of battles fought in the mid-19th century for "rights." These rights were important, and Elizabeth was sadly wrong in disassociating herself from the brave women who led the fight for them, but even more important was the philosophy underlying feminism with which she was not well acquainted and yet toward which her own life experience as a woman steadily propelled her. Her writings—both poetic and in her letters—are full of confusion and contradictions. She saw very clearly what was wrong with how the society of her day was organized, how the infamous double-standard operated, but much less clearly what needed to be done about it. She failed, for example, to see the vital role education could play, even going so far as to say she believed the majority of women's minds *were* weaker than the majority of men's and very little could be done about the discrepancy. Her own position had been immensely privileged and she considered any woman who tried hard enough and had the right sort of mind could educate herself as she had done. The idea that, no matter how good the mind there had to be access to the materials before any education could result, was foreign to her. If she had lived only a little longer she might well have been as dumbfounded as everyone else when the educational reforms initiated in the last quarter of the 19th century began to take effect. Always ready to widen her horizons, Elizabeth was not hostile to change, only sometimes slow to see where it could be made and although stubborn by nature she was never too proud to change her own mind.

Women can find in both the work and life of Elizabeth Barrett Browning more than men can. The echoes, for us, are repeated and deafening and remind me that where feminism is concerned it is indeed true that, as so many people have said, the same battles need to be fought *all over again* each generation. Every woman who falls in love and marries and bears a child has to wonder what it will do to her drive, her ambition, and her determination to be and do everything regardless. Feminists can, and do, argue 'til the cows come home about the existence of any "biological urge," some saying it exists to be conquered, others that it is all nonsense. Elizabeth Barrett certainly felt herself only half the woman she knew she could be until she found Robert Browning to love and when she did find him the release this brought her fuelled her to far greater heights than she had ever attained before. This may seem a dire message to draw from her life, depending on one's standpoint, but I find it inspirational. Which woman, after all, wants to believe her creativity will end if she succumbs to marriage and motherhood? (Who, on the other hand, wants to believe it will never really flourish *until* she does?) There is more to Elizabeth Barrett Browning's life than a sickly love story; it has in it all the ingredients of the classic female dilemma. "Woman to woman" is not the only way to approach it but it is certainly the way to get the best out of it from the biographer's point of view. The study of feminism brings to this biographer at least an awareness of motives and challenges which it would otherwise be impossible to relate to and has been of the greatest advantage. This is not to say that men cannot write biographies of women as well as women can—which would not only be sexist as well as ridiculous—but that men will have to verse themselves in feminism before they can write women's biographies, while women have it easier: They, in themselves, recognize and answer the echoes instinctively.

REFERENCES

Besier, Rudolf (1930). *The Barretts of Wimpole Street.* Boston, MA: Little, Brown & Co.

Barrett, Elizabeth B. (1820). *The battle of Marathon. A poem.* (Printed for Private Circulation, W. Lindsell.)

Browning, Elizabeth Barrett (1989). *Aurora Leigh.* Chicago, IL: Academy Chicago Pubs. Ltd.

Browning, Elizabeth Barrett (1986). *Sonnets from the Portugese: A Celebration of Love.* New York: St. Martin.

Browning, Elizabeth Barrett (1954). *Sonnets from the Portugese and Other Love Poems.* New York: Doubleday.

Foster, Margaret (1989). *Elizabeth Barrett Browning.* New York: Doubleday & Co., Inc.

Hicks, Malcolm (1983). *Selected Poems.* New York: Carcanet Press.

Kelley, Philip & Hudson, Ronald, Eds. (1984). *Brownings' Correspondence, Volume 1: 1809–1826.* Winfield, KS: Wedgestone Press.

Kelley, Philip & Hudson, Ronald, Eds. (1984). *Brownings' Correspondence, Volume 2: 1827–1831.* Winfield, KS: Wedgestone Press.

Kelley, Philip & Hudson, Ronald, Eds. (1985). *Brownings' Correspondence, Volume 3: 1832–1837.* Winfield, KS: Wedgestone Press.

Kelley, Philip & Hudson, Ronald, Eds. (1986). *Brownings' Correspondence, Volume 4: 1838–1840.* Winfield, KS: Wedgestone Press.

Kelley, Philip & Hudson, Ronald, Eds. (1987). *Brownings' Correspondence, Volume 5: 1841–1842*. Winfield, KS: Wedgestone Press.

Kelley, Philip & Hudson, Ronald, Eds. (1988). *Brownings' Correspondence, Volume 6: 1842–1842*. Winfield, KS: Wedgestone Press.

Kelley, Philip & Hudson, Ronald, Eds. (1989). *Brownings' Correspondence, Volume 7: 1843 Letters 1174–1406*. Winfield, Wedgestone Press.

Raymond, Meredith B. & Sullivan, Mary R., eds. (1983). *The Letters of Elizabeth Barrett Browning to Mary Russell Mitford, 1936–1854* (3 volumes). Winfield, KS: Wedgestone Press.

Chapter 13

Finding the Sources: Selling Women's Biography

Elizabeth Crawford

It is now a generally received opinion that women's history, having been lost or, in fact, never having existed, is being recovered. Those of us who took history at a university, even in the relatively enlightened days of the late 1960s, could pursue courses entitled "Social and Economic History" and never hear mention of women, save only in terms of the relative number of domestic servants and factory workers. No—history was a masculine subject, concerned with the interests of politicians, farmers, factory workers: men who were out in the world doing things. In political history, women's fight for the vote was a brief addendum to the long haul of Chartism and the 19th century Reform Acts.

I dimly perceived that "history" was a package of facts, to be selected and rearranged to fit the pattern of the moment. I had read E. H. Carr's (1961) *What is History?* and did realize that Sir Arthur Bryant and Eric Hobsbawn each used "history" for their own very different ends. But, while coasting through 3 years of facts, I never thought that, for me, what was missing was "women's history." Still so conditioned by a traditional upbringing and education, I was unable to use the tools that that education should have been forging. However, during all this time, for pleasure, I devoured the biographies, autobiographies, diaries, and journals of women. Women who were, necessarily, in history, written about, preserved on the library shelf, but not part of "history."

The last 20 years has seen the "discovery" and legitimization of women's history and literature, which are now quite indispensable components of courses in higher education. I would, incidentally, be most interested to read a history of this discovery, of how a subject is legitimized. Does it stem from one paper read at one convention, one journal article, the slow drip wearing away at the stone? Or does it result from a concerted assault on the academic fortress? Apart from women's history per se, the emphasis appears to have moved from the economic to the social side of "Social and Economic History"—or at least the previous imbalance has been rectified. Society is half female and that half has traditionally had charge of homes, bodies, childbirth, and children: all the rites of passage, the social glue. Information about women's lives, homes, children, and relations with parents, husbands, and friends are not found in state papers or Hansard (verbatim transcript of the proceedings of the House of Commons), but in the details that women themselves leave behind of their lives. These, for earlier periods, may be buried in family archives and in household accounts, but the richest seam of information is to be found in their autobiographies, biographies, diaries, and journals. Women's history was never "lost." As with their literature, it was there all the time waiting to be mined.

Through the last 20 years I have maintained and developed my interest in women's lives, much heartened by the spate of essays and monographs published in the late 1970s and 1980s. The first I read were *Relative Creatures: Victorian Women in Society and the Novel* by Françoise Basch (1974); *A Widening Sphere: Changing Roles of Victorian Women* (1977) and *Suffer and Be Still: Women in the Victorian Age* (1972), both edited by Martha Vicinus, followed quickly by *Feminist Theorists: Three Centuries of Women's Intellectual Traditions* (1983) edited by Dale Spender; *Strong-Minded Women* (1982) edited by Janet Horowitz Murray; *A Literature of Their Own: British Women Novelists From Brontë to Lessing* (1982) by Elaine Showalter; and *A Very Great Profession: The Woman's Novel, 1912–1939* (1983) by Nicola Beauman. All these books contain extensive, and, to me, thrilling, bibliographies. I felt a real compulsion to hunt for the original source material used in these studies and, of course, many of them are the biographies and autobiographies that I had been reading for pleasure for a long time. I felt a real sense of vindication in seeing them being given academic recognition.

When an opportunity arose to branch out into a new career, I realized that I could combine business with pleasure and justify the volume of my reading by selling books that would be of interest to those researching and studying women's history and literature. Having found little demand for books about nonBritish women I must, at the risk of appearing distinctly parochial, confine my observations to the reading and selling of biographies of British women.

I do find that I sell women's biographies mainly as tools for research. That, I am sure, does not preclude them also being read for pleasure, but I have been quite surprised that there is not more interest from lay readers, such as myself. I suppose that I am aiming at those who, having read either a new or republished study that has enjoyed the benefit of the able marketing skills of a feminist press, are prepared to delve a little deeper into the undergrowth of history and biography, rather than following only the now well-signposted route through the beautifully presented paperbacks on the "Women's Studies" shelves. I have a theory that it would do us all good to read of other peoples' lives. Academics engaged in research on individual women obviously need to read the existing autobiographies or biographies of their subject as a precursor to a fresh interpretation. Today's biographer approaches her subject carrying her own baggage of theories, experiences, and knowledge of "facts," and produces a very different study from that written, say, at the beginning of this century. The change in historical and cultural viewpoint throws women's lives into a new relief. Although such women as, at random, Charlotte Charke (in the 18th century) and Elizabeth Robins (in the early 20th century) wrote autobiographies, I would be delighted to read now of their lives from a late 20th century standpoint. Apart from interpreting her subject's life through her own experience, the biographer of today does have the invaluable facility of hindsight and can show the networks and interconnections surrounding her subject with a clarity not available to a contemporary of the subject. This is an aspect of biography that particularly appeals to me and one that has, I feel, not yet come into its own. Biographies and autobiographies have, on the whole, been the story of individuals as though they existed, if not entirely in a vacuum, at least in a world where life and achievements were of their own determining—the biography of achievement. I like the current approach that shows the principal as molded by others, as others are molded by her—perhaps the "cog" principle of biography—as expounded by Ann Morley and Liz Stanley (1988) in *The Life and Death of Emily Wilding Davison.*

Those researching general areas of interest, such as birth control, or parent–child relationships, or women's life-cycles through the ages, rely on autobiographical and biographical material for their primary sources. Many of the biographies of, say, 19th century women, published originally because they were the wives, daughters, or sisters of great men of the day, are being studied now not to see how they reacted to the issues of their time, but to find out at what intervals they produced their children, what they might do to prevent conception, how they arranged their children's education, and how they organized their households. A great deal of research is being undertaken to study the ways in which women in the past have broken from the way of life that was traditionally ordained for them. For instance, biographies of women educationalists, the late-19th-century and early-20th-century headmistresses, are always in demand. Some of these contemporary biographies may seen to us embarrassingly reverential and sentimental, but I feel that it is by noting this tone that one puts a finger on the pulse of the period. Headmistresses, presumably because of their ease with the pen, were quite prolific autobiographies. Women doctors were less so—and biographies of them are at a premium. Nurses were even less likely to leave behind formal biographies and autobiographies. All the research that has recently been done on women's work in the World Wars has drawn on nurses' unpublished reminiscences and diaries; perhaps nursing in wartime did attract the girls who were likely to put their lives on paper. Or it gave a chance of "doing something" to girls who had previously been well educated to do nothing such as Vera Brittain. Lives of women at war are generally good sellers. My favorite is a slim autobiography of a woman bus conductor, *"Clippie:" The Autobiography of a War-Time Conductress* (Z. Katin, 1944). Biographies of women social reformers and factory inspectors are always in demand but were originally published in small print runs, presumably because they were thought to be of little general interest, and are now, consequently, quite difficult to find.

The fight for the vote produced a spate of riveting autobiographies, both at the time and, like those by Mary Richardson (1953) and Cicely Hale (1973), up to 40 or 50 years later. Interestingly enough, very few of the main protagonists, the Pankhursts always excepted, have had fresh interpretative biographies written about them and so the autobiographies are required reading for those who want to unravel the many threads that finally led to women's enfranchisement. The history of women's suffragism is the history of those involved in the movement. By reading a fair number of these autobiographies it is especially interesting to unravel, as Liz Stanley (1985) has done for Olive Schreiner in *Feminism and Friendship* the webs of friendship that existed between so many superficially disparate women.

In each catalogue of second-hand and out-of-print books I produce, the biography section is dominated by the lives of women writers. The reason for this is self-evident. I can only sell those lives that are available to me. Writing was, and is, a sphere in which women have long been prolific. Writing was one of the few modes of self-expression available to them that could be undertaken at home in the bosom of the family. From the early beginnings, when Fanny Burney was shamed by thoughts of her father's putative displeasure into burning her first attempt at a novel (Judy Simons, 1987), women writers, often through financial necessity, gathered strength. As has so often been pointed out, the pen was one of the few tools available to the literate woman in the 18th and 19th centuries. The pen, although it might depict the world and its ways, did not necessitate direct contact with it and women writers did not compromise their characters as did, for instance, actresses. The epistolary form of the early novel was the style in which women were well practiced. Women at home carried on the tradition of reading and story telling to their children. If their husbands failed them, if their brothers were dissolute, women could at least attempt to earn their living by writing novels. The 19th century saw a great increase in the demand for novels; the circulating libraries made their dissemination increasingly wider. Many of these women novelists dashed off an autobiography between novels; the lives of such women as Mrs. Oliphant (Coghill, 1899), Mrs. Gaskell (Gérin, 1976), and Mrs. Humphry Ward (1918) tell us a great deal about the expectations and limitations of women's lives. Even though they were the main bread-winners and received some literary acclaim, they were beset by the domestic worries and crises that have been the lot of the family woman through the ages. As a contrast there is one collection of biographical articles about women writers that does present them in a rather different light. *Notable Women Authors of The Day* was edited by Helen Black and published in 1906. It contains interviews with 30 late Victorian authors, including Marie Corelli, Sarah Grand, Annie S. Swan, and Rhoda Broughton. These ladies are depicted as efficient career women, well able to maintain their literary production while organizing their households and living calm and ordered lives. All these autobiographies and biographies, however reverential, provide very useful source material on many aspects of the lives of a certain kind of working woman.

Women have always been inveterate journal keepers and letter writers. For instance, Fanny Burney wrote up to five letters every day for over 70 years, and 2,000 of these letters have survived (Simons, 1987). Many of the biographies of women in the 18th and 19th centuries are, indeed, collections of their letters, filled out with linking text. The fact that many of the biographies would with heartfelt justice be described as "pious" should not deter our interest. They were a product of their times and I do feel that these, and the "missionary" biographies of the late 19th century, have as yet been unfairly neglected. Women's journals and letters, dealing as they do with matters of life and death and all the impediments of day to day living in between, are indispensable to any study of previous societies. It is a revelation to see their lives come leaping off the page. It is in these that we see how a large part of the population lived—albeit the life of the literate classes.

On the whole the women's journals that have survived into print and general dissemination are those of women of character. The *Journeys of Celia Fiennes* (C. Morris, 1947) bring the 17th century to life as she surveys England with her reporter's eye. The Journals of Lady Mary Coke from 1756 to 1774 (see Coke, 1970) have long been one of my favorite sources of information on 18th-century life at court and in society. A little thing—it was from one of her days that I realized that in the 18th century time was necessarily an arbitrary affair. Her household clocks were several hours slow and she arrived at her sister's house to find that the expected meal had long been cleared away. Fanny Burney's journals are required reading. Through the diary that she kept for most of her long life (1752–1843) she breathes the past into life. There can be no better way of feeling what a real kind of life can have been like in that period than through reading her journals and letters. Admittedly, as with most women (or men, indeed) who wrote their own lives or have had them written, she is from the particular stratum of society that does wield the pen and does put its thoughts on paper; but, given that, she sees of life at all levels and knows what living is like.

Stepping, briefly, beyond these shores, I would like to draw attention to the *Journals of Madame de la Tour du Pin* (F. Harcourt, 1969). It was only by reading these that the French Revolution, which always cropped up in some guise or other in history and politics courses, fell into a perspective that to me made sense of the jigsaw pieces of fact. Rather than as a heroic canvas, slashed with slogans, the history of the period could be seen in miniature through her eyes as she coped with life in the turmoil. Although her own life was such a tiny part of the whole, it animated the period as no conventional histories ever had.

Although I sell biographies of women mainly to academics I have also noted recently that there has been a decided interest from actresses in the fringe theatre. There have recently been one-woman presentations of the lives of Sylvia Pankhurst; of Alexandra Kollantai; and of Constance Markievicz and Eva Gore-Booth. Women's lives can leap off the page onto the stage and there is a groundswell of interest in one-women biographical shows. I find this most heartening as it does lead to my final thesis. That is that women's biography gives strength. Spotlights on strong-minded and interesting women obviously help "The Cause" but a general revival of interest in women's lives would benefit us all. As I think that it is in the social trivia, the glue, the rites of passage, the coping with daily life that women's written lives excel, so I think that reading how women have managed in the past in very much harsher physical, social, and economic climates makes us take stock of our own lives. I certainly feel that life's troughs come as less of a shock if we know that generations before us have experienced the same situations and emotions. Can biographies give strength? Does the reading of the journals, letters, biographies, and autobiographies of our foremothers prepare us better for living our own lives? I think that it does. As you see I bring a certain missionary fervor to the selling of women's biographies.

NOTE

A fellow book-dealer has compiled and is publishing the first comprehensive listing of biographies of British women. All types of journals, memoirs, autobiographies, and lives and letters are included. The first volume is *The Victorian Woman: An Index to Biographies and Memoirs* by Peter Bell and is available from Elizabeth Crawford at 5 Owen's Row, London, EC1V 4NP. It will be followed by complementary indexes on the Regency Woman (c. 1780–c. 1830) and the Edwardian Woman (c. 1900–c. 1902).

REFERENCES

Basch, Françoise. (1974). *Relative creatures: Victorian women in society and the novel*. London: Allen Lane.

Beauman, Nicola. (1983). *A very great profession: The woman's novel 1914–1939*. London: Virago.

Black, Helen. (1906). *Notable women authors of the day*. Glasgow: Maclaren.

Carr, E. H. (1961). *What is history?* London: Macmillan.

Charke, Charlotte. (1929). *A narrative of the life of Mrs. Charlotte Charke*. London: Constable.

Coghill, Mrs H. (Ed.). (1899). *The autobiography and letters of Mrs M.O.W. Oliphant*. London: Blackwood & Sons.

Coke, Lady Mary. (1970). *Letters and journals, 1756–1774*. Bath: Kingsmead Reprints.

Gérin, Winifred. (1976). *Elizabeth Gaskell: A biography*. Oxford: Clarendon Press.

Hale, Cicely. (1973). *A good long time*. Brighton: Regency Press.

Harcourt, F. (Ed. & Trans.). (1969). *Journals of Madame de la Tour du Pin*. London: Harvill Press.

Katin, Z. (1944). *"Clippie:" The autobiography of a war-time conductress*. London: John Gifford.

Morley, Anne, & Stanley, Liz. (1988). *The life and death of Emily Wilding Davison*. London: Women's Press.

Morris, C. (Ed.). (1947). *Journeys of Celia Fiennes*. London: Cresset Press.

Murray, Janet Horowitz (Ed.). (1982). *Strong-minded women*. London: Penguin Books.

Richardson, Mary. (1953). *Laugh a defiance*. London: Weidenfeld & Nicolson.

Robins, Elizabeth. (1940). *Both sides of the curtain*. London: Heinemann.

Showalter, Elaine. (1982). *A literature of their own: British women novelists from Brontë to Lessing*. London: Virago.

Simons, Judy. (1987). *Fanny Burney*. London: Macmillan.

Spender, Dale (Ed.). (1983). *Feminist theorists: Three centuries of women's intellectual traditions*. London: Women's Press.

Stanley, Liz. (1985). *Feminism and friendship: Two essays on Olive Schreiner*. Manchester: Dept. of Sociology, University of Manchester.

Vicinus, Martha (Ed.). (1972). *Suffer and be still: Women in the Victorian age*. Bloomington, IN: Indiana University Press.

Vicinus, Martha (Ed.). (1977). *A widening sphere: Changing roles of Victorian women*. Bloomington, IN: Indiana University Press.

Ward, Mrs Humphry. (1918). *A writer's recollections*. London: Collins.

Ward, W. C. (Ed.). 1890. *The diary and letters of Madame d'Arblay (Frances Burney)*. London: Vizettely.

Part 5
Readers

There is a growing vocabulary of perspectives that can be brought to bear on each new women's biography that appears. It cannot be predicted how a particular reader will make the connections. Meanings can be created anew, and no test of validity can predict their range, their richness, their variety.

A powerful alchemy can work across time and place to address any woman who is drawn to a story in which her own reflection might be found. A reflection which both is and is not herself, yet which connects her with her own creative independence.

Liz Dearden chooses to approach her theme through the review of biographies by women who are themselves reviewers. Takayo Mukai has written a deeply sensitive account of her own learning as a girl, as a woman, and as a feminist, from reading women's biography.

Chapter 14

Reviewing Women's Biography

Liz Dearden

Wendy Mulford (1988): *This Narrow Place: Sylvia Townsend Warner and Valentine Ackland: A Life, Letters & Politics* 1930–1951.

Claire Tomalin (1988): *A Secret Life: A Biography of Katherine Mansfield*

Lyndall Gordon (1984/1986): *Virginia Woolf: A Writer's Life*

The choice of subject for review, like the choice of subject for biography, derives from autobiographical concerns; this acknowledgment of the subjective in the process of any writing is one of feminism's major contributions to critical theory. So the fact that the three biographies I have chosen to look at are all literary is a personal preference coupled with an intention to focus on writers who had relationships with one another's work, even if only tangentially. In addition, there is the pleasure of identifying with women who were all reviewers themselves and an attraction to positive role models—women who were not afraid to be opinionated or uncompromising and who set their own critical standards.

In many ways however, these are conventional biographical subjects—exceptional, famous, and talented—and as such resist current feminist trends toward documenting ordinary lives. Nevertheless, all the biographers felt that as women they had special empathy with their women subjects. In Wendy Mulford's (1988) case it was through her relationship with the house where Sylvia and Valentine lived and her relationship with Sylvia's close friend Antonia Trauttmansdorff, whose own memories preface the biography in a way which acknowledges multiple authorship. Both Claire Tomalin (1988) and Lyndall Gordon (1984/1986) believed they were revising and rewriting previous biographies which were only partial accounts. For instance, according to Phyllis Rose (1978/1986), Quentin Bell (1973) had left out altogether "a treatment of Woolf's writing, which is to say he omits much of her inner life apart from her madness" (Heilbrun, 1988). They were all concerned with the openness of biography to change or to what has been called its kaleidoscopic tendency the tendency of a life to be seen in different patterns by different people (Liz Stanley, 1987).

WENDY MULFORD

Dust jackets—the clothing of any text—entice or deflect our interest; they are our first impression just as when we meet new people we are influenced by how they look and what that may signal. The cover of Wendy Mulford's (1988) book represents not only a lively publishing house style of wraparound design, but also a postmodernist montage technique that involves a complex way of seeing. It illustrates also the process of writing biography, the searching out, selection and fabrication that makes up the text. Its "muddy" background and multiplicity of image has a disruptive dynamic that articulates something of the subversive political content of the lives of the two subjects. In this way the book declares itself to a certain market.

The paradigm that Wendy Mulford aspires to is a demanding one set out in a paper prepared for a conference on Writing Feminist Biography and entitled *In This Process I Too Am Subject* (1986); it articulates Wendy Mulford's primary commitment to the inevitability of personal involvement with the subject of biographical work. In her account of process she devotes considerable space to describing her unique experience of living in the house in Dorset where Sylvia and Valentine spent so much of their lives. For the biographer, then, her subjects live on in this materiality, whereas readers of Wendy Mulford, Sylvia Townsend Warner, and Valentine Ackland experience their continued presence only through their writing.

By deciding to write a double biography Wendy Mulford challenges a genre which usually privileges one individual's life above others, although she states that this was a change of direction that took place while work was already in progress, when she realized the arbitrariness inherent in the politics of publishing. Furthermore, her biography attempts to foreground the dialogue taking place between Sylvia and Valentine through their work, particularly through their collaborative experiment in poetry. Like Sylvia and Valentine, Wendy Mulford also works to find an appropriate voice, flirting with the possibility of new forms for biography and most importantly intending to use a language rooted in material conditions, in place, domesticity, and dailiness which will be accessible to as wide a readership as possible. Lastly, Wendy Mulford acknowledges that biography is in part fictional, and also that it is a fiction of biography to believe that the biographer can produce an objective, truthful account when the biographer is mediating lives through her own "freight of culture, class and consciousness" (Mulford, 1988).

The dual-stranded narrative of *This Narrow Place*—particularly in the early part of the book, which charts the two women's lives prior to their involvement with each other—is actually difficult to follow and reads as disjointed with uneasy, abrupt shifts from one life to another. This structural difficulty or awkwardness is resolved more successfully in the main body of the text where their lives and work are closely enmeshed. Wendy Mulford's intention to give both women's lives equal weight is a way of redressing a balance that had always been tipped in Sylvia's favor; Wendy Mulford thereby brings Valentine out of the shadows, out of the obscurity that history imposed on her because of her unlikeable personality, and possibly because of her overt sexual orientation. Wendy Mulford's recuperation of Valentine encourages readers to question the integrity of publishing policies determined by the amount of social acceptability of authors. We are made aware too, of Wendy Mulford's own dislike of Valentine and the problematic of trying to neutralize these feelings when assessing her work: "sometimes I consoled myself with the exchange between her [Sylvia Townsend Warner] and Virginia Woolf, they did not like each other, but Sylvia admired Virginia Woolf's work. 'Tell me Miss Warner,' said Virginia Woolf, 'How do you know so much about witches? Is it because you are one?' " (Mulford, 1988). Wendy Mulford has to confront the guilt associated with discovering role models that will not fit the mold we have made from them. In this way we are drawn into the subtext that investigates the need or wish of the biographer to like her subject, and the necessarily fictive way their life stories will be produced according to these wishes and fantasies. Furthermore, just as feeling toward the subject may change, there is also an awareness built in to the biography of the subject's constantly shifting position which frustrates the possibility of constructing a consistent portrait. Wendy Mulford chooses to focus on *Lolly Willowes* (Sylvia Townsend Warner, 1926) in her critical commentary because she locates in witchcraft a metaphor for the power of change in our lives through the reclamation of lost skills.

The interchapters of the biography, which constitute the critical commentary on each writer's work, fail to integrate with the life narrative; in fact, they serve to push the writers apart again. Having constructed their lives together, the amount of space given over to discussion of Syliva's work, in comparison with Valentine's, tends to reinforce positions on major and minor artists, published and unpublished. In addition, the voice of the commentary, particularly that on Sylvia Townsend Warner's fiction sounds like an academic essay which has been inserted to bulk out the text. It is unclear why Wendy Mulford chooses to place such dense textual analysis between sections of the narrative. The temptation is to skip over them completely, which defeats the object of trying to establish the seamlessness of life and work. Like Sylvia Townsend Warner and Valentine Ackland, Wendy Mulford is experimenting with new form for her approaches to biography. To a certain extent this justifies the unevenness of the text, which echoes the uneven trajectory of women's lives as their experience rejects the linear progression associated with a goal-orientated career. On the other hand, I feel drawn to take up Virginia Woolf's uncompromisingly critical position, that as women we have to learn not to be conciliatory as reviewers, to not accept uncritically feminist approaches but to test them against other works in their genre and arrive at an honest assessment. To be fair to Wendy Mulford, by choosing to focus on the intimate relationship between Sylvia and Valentine she was taking on not only the lesbophobia of the publishing world but also the restrictions and prohibitions imposed on her by the executors of Sylvia Townsend Warner's estate. To be haunted by a withheld body of material did however propel her toward a more intuitive or fictionalized biography; it also draws our attention to the way the legal system controls access to documents to make sure that the "right" or acceptable version is produced.

The third strand of Wendy Mulford's work concentrates on the political milieu and provides a fascinating insight into the realities of grassroots work with Left Review and the Communist Party; this work is epitomized by Sylvia's letter to Nancy Cunard in 1944 summing up her belief that there is another sort of war, a civil war that "will come and must come before the world can begin to grow up, will be fought out on this terrain of man and woman." She was in other words, privileging gender over class, a perception that may be commonplace in feminism now but in the 1930s was new and still controversial.

Unfortunately, the quality of the illustrations in Wendy Mulford's book is poor because they are not reproduced on better quality paper; however, they are not bunched together as in more traditional texts but are distributed evenly throughout the book. These photographs speak of the centrality of place in Sylvia and Valentine's lives and speak also out of what Griselda Pollock (1988) called the "spaces of femininity," the interiors of houses, private gardens, and terraces. They read like snapshots from any family album except that these are images almost without exception of one by the other and none of them provide a pictorial record of the two women together, apart from the one with Julius Lipton. From the photographs we pick up clues about clothing and its crucial role in defining the self; Valentine's love of style is self-evident as she habitually wears trousers and jodhpurs with immaculate shirts and ties. In these types of clothing she stares defiantly at the camera standing self-consciously posed in a formal way. Sylvia, on the other hand, favors skirts and blouses or light summer dresses, has a softer hairstyle, and by contrast is nearly always sitting and often absorbed in some activity such as reading, playing with pets, or sewing. The one formal publicity portrait depicts her looking pensive and studious—the serious lady novelist stereotype. It could be argued that these images fuel preconceptions about lesbians adopting "masculine" or "feminine" roles; the text absolutely refutes this, but equally the images underwrite the personalities which emerge from the text: the insecurity of Valentine manifested as posturing and egotistical vanity and the easy going and less "driven" personality of Sylvia manifested through her relaxed engagement with her environments. The myth of happiness that snapshots perpetuate is partially deconstructed by less positive notes which creep into one or two of the images, particularly the one where Valentine stands "caged" behind the chestnut palings, looking anxious and melancholic with her hands behind her back as if she were hiding something; the reader tends to supply the whisky bottle!

CLAIRE TOMALIN

Claire Tomalin's (1988) biography of Katherine Mansfield appears to be a more conventional approach and is an expectation set up by its subtitle, *A Secret Life,* which draws the reader in with a promise of revelation. In a recent radio interview about biography, Claire Tomalin gave an indication of what it is that informs her work: Like Wendy Mulford she acknowledges the fictional element and in particular she is interested in imagining what the subject might have been if circumstances had been different. She declares an interest in the importance of the outsider figure together with a belief that she is producing the best version that can be done at a particular time, realizing that subsequent material will produce a revision or something different. In addition Claire Tomalin carries the conviction that as a woman she will bring to her subject an understanding she feels has been absent in previous biographies of Katherine Mansfield.

The emphasis Claire Tomalin places on the idea of secrecy is not so much the withheld part of the writer's personality or "the submerged," which is so integral to an understanding of Virginia Woolf, but a facet of a woman who everyone, including her biographer, concludes was fundamentally deceptive and untrustworthy. The discovery of her secrets, the penetration of the privacy she constructed around herself is very much at the heart of the book, and in this it fulfills a hunger for revelation which functions to make us as readers secure. The word "secret" is applied by Claire Tomalin to the poverty of which Katherine Mansfield was ashamed, her autobiography which she had only just begun, the plagiarism which her lover Floryan was accused of encouraging, and the medical facts of her disease which Claire Tomalin calls one of Floryan's "poisoned gifts." What Katherine Mansfield was hiding, Claire Tomalin uses to help explain someone who acted out a role of "bad behavior" and social unacceptability; in many ways it does mitigate her apparently unlovable characteristics. Claire Tomalin's detailed description, however, of Katherine's medical condition tends toward morbidity and reads like Victorian medical discourse, which defines woman through her body alone.

The photograph chosen for the cover underwrites this view of Katherine Mansfield: It is black and white, sombre and painful, betraying her illness and imminent death. Although constructed in a classical way—side lit with a three quarter face cropped to head and shoulder—it nevertheless refuses illusion and in its emotional intensity is close to the spirit of Jo Spence's (1986) work on documenting the diseased body. Similarly, the photograph, on the back of the dust cover, of Katherine Mansfield and John Middleton Murry speaks of the dislocation and difficulty which was a feature of their relationship to the end; again there is no attempt to idealize them. Perhaps the "truth" of these images resides in who took them. In fact, they were both taken by the faithful Ida Baker, Katherine's secret confidante and "wife," illustrating a point made by Victor Burgin (1984) that "a photograph is a record of a reality refracted through a sensibility: what I see is something seen the way someone else saw it."

These photographs articulate the downward trajectory of Katherine's life caused by physical disintegration. But would Katherine have approved, herself such a consummate liar, of such an "untouched-up" version of herself? It is probable she would have raged against it in the way she quarrelled so violently with John Middleton Murry over a photograph he gave Constables for the jacket of one of her books!

The photographs taken of Katherine before the First World War tell a different story and contextualize her in her various London homes. One is of Katherine Mansfield in the Chaucer Mansions flat where she and Murry had to move in order to clear debts: There is a starkness about the room that draws the eye first to Katherine's extraordinary sidelong glance avoiding the gaze of the camera, then back to the buddha and hookah on the mantelpiece, and down to the reflection of the bowl of primroses in the highly polished surface of her dining room table—Katherine's workspace as John Middleton Murry had commandeered the living room for his study. In fact, Katherine Mansfield moved house endlessly; the sensation of someone moving very fast through life, restless, without roots and "observing with a stranger's eye" is mirrored in Claire Tomalin's narrative which has a similar pace, moving from one episode or drama to the next as Katherine hurtles toward her death. The impermanence of Katherine Mansfield's lifestyle is used by Claire Tomalin as a key to understand Katherine's facility for taking people up as intimate friends, then passing on and not bothering to keep up with them. Parallels are also drawn with her short stories, which have the same flavor of dropping in on places and lives and then moving on without trace. The speed and intensity of the charting of Katherine's Mansfield's life draws attention to Katherine's rapidly changing sense of self, documented in a page of photographs titled "The Changing Face of Katherine Mansfield." Claire Tomalin reveals the extent of Katherine's ambivalence not only toward herself but also toward other people, houses, and her mother. Her sexual ambiguity is also revealed which, in turn, reveals Claire Tomalin's ambivalence toward this side of Katherine's life; the tone of the writing becomes moralistic, with the use of loaded words such as "disordered," "aberrant," "perverted," and "delinquent" which are difficult to detach from the biographer. As Katherine herself grew older she ironically became almost puritanical about "corruption."

Claire Tomalin's insistence on change and movement denies the possibility of imposing a coherent pattern onto a life and projects her reader towards imagining the "might have beens" of Katherine Mansfield's life had her career not been so sadly curtailed.

LYNDALL GORDON

Lyndall Gordon's (1984) biography of Virginia Woolf's life addresses itself primarily to the correspondence between Virginia Woolf's life as it fed into her writing. Lyndall Gordon's textual analysis illustrates how Virginia Woolf as a writer of fiction was constantly "doing biography" herself. Virginia Woolf's theories about biography rested on a belief in an intuitive approach to a subject, letting the imagination tease out of a life its decisive moments or "moments of being." Just as we have seen Claire Tomalin try to locate those decisive moments in the life of Katherine Mansfield, Lyndall Gordon works with Virginia Woolf in the same way.

The cover of Lyndall Gordon's book, with its Bloomsbury-inspired colors and central portrait of Virginia painted by her sister, reinforces Lyndall Gordon's suggestion that both women were engaged in fictional biography and also points to the centrality of the relationship between the sisters which Virginia Woolf called their "private nucleus." Its sea greens and slightly murky quality, in conjunction with the familiar "submerged" look of Virginia's eyes as they stare passively outside the frame absorbing light and sensation, speak of Vanessa's intimate knowledge of her sister's need for a kind of private receptivity in order to write.

Where Claire Tomalin draws a portrait of a writer whose transience fuelled an art rooted in the episodic moment with its own fragile poignancy, Lyndall Gordon draws a portrait of a writer for whom domestic stability created the still pool from which her work surfaced. It is impossible to review either their biographies or their work in isolation as they had a professional fascination with each other verging on compulsion—inspiring one another, making one another jealous, having at times an instinctive empathy over childhood trauma and the loss of brother and sister. Lyndall Gordon places greater emphasis on Virginia's relationship with Katherine than previous biographers who have concentrated instead on Vita Sackville-West.

The context Claire Tomalin puts her subject in is masculinist with its ambitions, competition, and literary rivalries, and it is not until Katherine arrives at the Villa Isola Bella at the end of her life that her persistent fantasy of a home in the country is realized. This "first real home of my own I've ever loved" (Tomalin, 1988) inspired her to write about the natural world with great clarity in her letters to John Middleton Murry. But Isola Bella was an isolated and exiled domesticity necessitated by Katherine's ill-health. The environment of Sussex and Bloomsbury was communal and open, which nourished moments of sublimity located in the domestic scene. Lyndall Gordon recognizes that an integral part of Virginia's inventiveness was in contriving this "feminised setting" where painting and writing had priority, entertaining was informal, and interior decoration innovative. Like Virginia Woolf, Lyndall Gordon has a sensitivity that allows her to discover what is interesting about a writer's life that is without public action, and instead "vibrates" (one of Virginia's favorite words) with "invisible presences." Like Virginia Woolf, she is not afraid to have gaps or silences in her text—she jumps from discussing Virginia Woolf at 40 to Virginia Woolf at 50—because she traces not literal passing of time but the links between moments of psychic importance. As readers we insert the unsaid into the text: the clutter of everyday life, the moments of nonbeing. The centrality of Virginia Woolf's family and friends to her writing has dictated the choice of photographs. As in Wendy Mulford's book, the locations are spatially specific to femininity, the house and garden, apart from the extraordinary statuesque picture taken from a very low angle, giving Virginia Woolf a powerful presence. It has a soft grainy texture, like weathered stone, and it complements Lyndall Gordon's sculptural phrase, "she pared away the foliage of personality to glimpse the rocks beneath" (1984/1986, p. 234). Virginia Woolf, unlike Katherine Mansfield, is pictured in a very social context, captured in the middle of conversation or gesture or, in portraits, is represented in her better known remote and pensive mood, which contrasts so dramatically with her animation in social settings. Lyndall Gordon perceives both sides of Virginia's personality and gives them equal attention as she concludes that Virginia Woolf needed both the stimulation of a busy social life and her reflective time set apart from it. Her approach to Virginia Woolf does much to redress a balance that has straitjacketed Virginia Woolf in popular imagination as the upper class, mad woman dependent on a supportive husband, a view of her which the biography by Quentin Bell (1973) tends to sustain.

CONCLUSION

There is a sense in which these reviews perform a different function from a review of a newly published work where the reviewer's position is powerfully influential as some sort of arbiter of public taste in reading. Here, I have demonstrated through comparison the relationship between biographies as they challenge the genre with their differing approaches. From the perspective of a novice at reviewing I would like to point out that the process of writing this chapter has confirmed me in the belief that anyone can be in a position of authority. As readers we have been schooled to expect or need to be told what to think, and it is easy to be seduced into accepting other people's critical assessments. A feminist methodology with its commitment to collaborative authorship works against the hierarchies of critical authority in an attempt to encourage readers to be confident of their own critical ability and to discourage passive acceptance of established opinion.

REFERENCES

Bell, Quentin. (1973). *Virginia Woolf: A biography*. London: Hogarth Press.
Burgin, Victor. (1984). *Screen, 25*(1).
Gordon, Lyndall. (1984/1986). *Virginia Woolf: A writer's life*. Oxford: Oxford University Press.
Heilbrun, Carolyn. (1988). *Writing a woman's life*. London: Women's Press.
Mulford, Wendy. (1988). *This narrow place: Sylvia Townsend Warner and Valentine Ackland. A life letters, & politics, 1930–1951*. London: Pandora.
Mulford, Wendy. (1986/1987). *In this process I too am subject*. Studies in Sexual Politics, *13* & *14*, Manchester University.
Pollock, Griselda. (1988). *Vision and difference*. London: Routledge.
Rose, Phyllis. (1978/1986). *Woman of letters: A life of Virginia Woolf*. London: Pandora.
Rose, Phyllis. (1985). *Writing on women, essays in a renaissance*. Middletown: Wesleyan University Press.
Spence, Jo. (1986). *Putting myself in the picture*. London: Camden Press.
Stanley, Liz. (1987). Biography as a microscope or kaleidoscope. *Women's Studies International Forum, 10*(1). London: Pergamon.
Tomalin, Claire. (1988). *A secret life: A biography of Katherine Mansfield*. London: Penguin Books.
Townsend Warner, Sylvia. (1926). *Lolly Willowes*. London: Chalto & Windus.

Chapter 15
Learning from Women's Biography

Takayo Mukai

We change. Touching the walls, we prepare to pounce. Here, doors lead into doors. There are rooms disappearing behind us! (Maggie Anderson, 1973, p. 9)

When she was a little girl, she adopted a role that fitted neatly with a nickname she happened to like, otenba—a tomboy.

There was a warning on the corridor of the elementary school; "Do Not Run," which she kept ignoring.

When the boy who sat next to her tried everything he could in order to make her cry, she cast him away instead.

When all the girls in the biology lab were scared to cut a small fish, she stood up and took a knife.

She was not scared. She was not "just like a girl." She was "honored" to play with boys. She was not inferior to boys (like other girls were). She was different. She was "exceptional."

"Grown-ups" told each other that she would make a doctor or a lawyer or a diplomat . . . only if she were a boy. Too bad. Sorry for her parents. She will have a hard time to find a man, though.

Well, let's see.

She did not become a doctor.

Nor a lawyer.

Nor a business executive.

They were right. She is not married.

She is now everything that her parents wished her not be be 20 years ago.

Not a few people asked me one simple question. "What had brought you into feminism?" Although I have tried countless times to answer this question, I am still no expert at it. I am far from being one. Instead, I stumble. Mumble. Feeling for "right" words which would hopefully enfold a part of me, "that" part of me . . . when I was a little girl. When I simply believed that everything would be possible only if I tried hard enough, and if I was good enough it would not matter whether I were a girl or a boy. When I did not know that my being female matters more than my being good or not.

I grew up in the countryside of Japan, where women's lives have not changed very much for generations, where baby girls are not as welcome as baby boys, where a married woman without a baby could still be called "umazume"—a stone woman—and, carry the punishment throughout their lives. My family was not particularly a conservative one, with a mother working full time, and her husband who shared half of the housework. I did not grow up with this image in TV dramas where fathers (husbands) sat and uttered only nouns: tea, newspaper, and bath. I was lucky in that.

My parents, when I look back, seemed to have encouraged me to learn as much as I wished to, partially because, I figure, they did not have a son (in a culture where boys usually get more attention as well as practical support from the family). I do not recall many occasions when I was told to do or not to something because I was a girl. Later, however, I often wondered if I had had a brother, would it have affected some of the decisions that I had made in my life, or at least my parents' approval (or disapproval) of them.

I do not remember when exactly was the first time that I heard the word "women's lib." I had known the word for a few years before I understood what it meant literally and it was years later again that I actually experienced the significance of the reality as well as the context in which the word was alive. I had grown up, accepting the societal notion that girls are inferior to boys in every way except being a wife and a mother. To be precise, it was not even a matter of acceptance. As Mary Daly put it, my mind was set, bound within a framework in which it was "true" that female meant "of less value" and that was the way it was (Mary Daly, 1978, pp. 1–34). I had never questioned why, then, female meant inferior or why they said it was better for a girl to be pretty than to be smart. Because I was unaware of the external structure that devalued women into objects in the future marriage market, I therefore did not care about the situation in which women were forced to be so. Everything was fine as long as only "I" was exempt from the dumping, was "exceptional," and was given chances to compete with boys. I was arrogant, without knowing that I was despising my own group of people, devaluing half of human experiences, and above all, I was ignorant of the invisible barriers between other women and myself by joining (although not really being accepted into) a "superior" group.

My encounter with feminism was itself a process, a journey which is still going on, a journey that had already started even before I found myself to be on it, and a journey that keeps carrying me along, through rooms.

There was always one popular question whenever little girls got together. "What would you like to be when you grow up?" And there were a few ever-presenting answers with ever-presenting smiles and widened eyes. A nurse. A babysitter. A wife. A mother . . .

Because she had replied differently each time she was invited to answer, she does not remember in what order she said what or how she said them. For one time, the answer was a pianist, followed by a writer or a translator or something of the sort.

She never wished that she were a boy. Because, she thought, it was more fun to be a girl and to be as good as boys, rather than just being a boy. That would be less exciting. Nothing special. No fun.

She enjoyed reading. Especially reading biographies, stories of people whose lives were "chosen" to be shared.

About what they accomplished, and how.

How courageous they were.

How talented they were.

How dedicated they were to their callings . . .

She was fascinated by their adventures, their achievements, but never wondered how these peoples' lives had turned into books, or what made them "great." She had never thought about others whose lives never made a book. Nor why not.

She came back to the corner of the school library again and again. To that corner where the "world biography series for children" sat, neatly and attractively.

It had never occurred to her that "these people" were all male.

That a biography series of "great men in the world" did not include the female, as the word "men" was supposed to (Dale Spender, 1980, pp. 151–154).

That those who were courageous, talented, and dedicated were males, a group of "men" to which she did not belong.

It was much later that she realized that everybody and everything in the world had been telling her not to expect too much. Not to be ambitious. Because they wanted her to be "happy," to be "safe," to stay where she was. Not to take any risks.

Because she was a girl.

It was much later that she realized that the world does not expect a girl to be as competent as boys. Girls grow up to be wives and mothers but not to be "successful" or "selected."

Then, doubts and questions and wonders flooded into her.

Aren't there any "great" women in the world?

If not, why not? If there were, why haven't they been chosen for biographies?

What have women been doing? Where have they gone?

If she could not be one of those great "men," she could at least be a great "woman," more precisely, an "exceptional" woman. She wanted to know how. She turned to the lives of women who were "extraordinary," looking for a role model, only to find a gap between their lives and her ongoing life, only to realize that they did not stand on a common ground (Susan Armitage, 1987, pp. 1–4). (Or at least that was the way the story—the language—had described the lives of "great" women.) What had constituted "events" in her daily life—failure, mother, boys, periods, future—were simply not there. Instead, the lives of "great women" seemed to be so colorfully scattered with talents, luck, efforts, and courage that brought success eventually in spite of the fact that they were female. Stories talked about why these lives were worth being recorded. The subjects of stories were not "women." There was no place for their lives and hers to meet.

She was disappointed.

She felt rejected.

She found herself with an urge for the knowledge of other women's lives. It was in a way like wanting to know about new female friends.

How did she grow up? What was her childhood like? Did she enjoy school? What interested her? How did she make decisions in her life? How did she survive through hardships? What made her happy or unhappy?

It did not matter whether the woman was an "exceptional" woman or not. Because it was no longer the extraordinariness of the genius that fascinated her. Rather, it was the "ordinariness" even in the lives of "exceptional" women that brought her closer to the subjects, to her new friends.

I had moved out of one room. A roomful of "great men"—Beethoven, Mozart, Edison, Nobel. . . . Men whom I knew only in their portraits, nicely framed and hung on the walls. Then I moved into a room where I was introduced to "exceptional women"—Umeko Tsuda, Helen Keller, and Margaret Mead. And to another room where the door is always open, to any women, famous or not, distinguished or not, where they all come out of the frames, sit next to me and talk to me, hand in hand, just like close friends would do. The distant and hierarchal relationship that I used to have with those who were "great" had disappeared. It had transformed. The women I met in biographies and whom I used to look up to from far away are now friends of mine who smile, cry, hesitate, and protest with me. They invited me into their lives in order to share not only their accomplishments but rather, more crucially, their pains and sufferings. Our lives are now interwoven. My mind is no longer bound. We reached over to each other, across the boundaries of cultures, historical periods, and socioeconomic classes, and, most of all, across the nets with which the patriarchy tries to entrap us and divide us into categories.

There are many lives that crisscrossed mine. Some have gone for years. Some stayed and became good friends. Among those who had enough patience with me, I would like to talk about Diane Arbus here. Our friendship has been one of those between women, with occasional shifts, turns, and returns, but we never abandon each other.

It has been 6 years since I got to know Diane through a photojournalist, Ruiko Yoshida. After making my first impression of this interesting creative photographer, I forgot about her completely for several years.

I was living in Japan and was a college sophomore, majoring in something in which I could not see my future, suffocated, sparing as much time as possible on my independent reading. I was reading a lot of women's works, regardless of the field. I was, when I look back from now, looking for that segment where our lives—other women's and mine—met and intersected. I was no longer concerned about how I wished to fulfill my potential in men's world, in a socially recognizable world. I was more eager to find out what made me comfortable, what made me true to myself, as a woman, in a way other than in the usually socially defined sense, but in my own way of experiencing (and enjoying) the fact.

Ironically, however, the works and lives of women that I turned to were not those of "ordinary" women. The very availability of their work (a portion of their lives) had inevitably distinguished them from the rest of women whose lives and experiences I wished to relate to. I wanted to know private lives of women, the very makings of their beings, which was accessible only through what had been made visible in public, what had been legitimized to be of worth. I was unaware of this dilemma even though I had started to refer to myself as a feminist. I was dying for something like a mirror or a contact sheet reflected on somebody else's life that would not only validate but also empower my way of being.

I came to be fascinated by Ruiko Yoshida's work, in which I came across her interaction with Diane Arbus. I had never seen Diane's work before. I was not sure if it was available in Japan or not.

In her brief memoir, Ruiko (1983) talked about her own association of Diane's life with that of a female character in a film they had seen together. Diane had terminated her marriage which had lasted 20-some years and had started photographing on her own people in the "dark world." A women in the film was about Diane's age, single, successful in her career, however, when her first affair had to be ended, she killed herself in despair, which was the last scene of the film. Even after the light was on, Diane, recalls Ruiko, did not move, looking into the dead screen, without a word, in a pale, expressionless face. A few years later when Ruiko received the call that Diane had killed herself, she could not get Diane's pale face and trembling lips out of her mind. Ruiko suspected Diane's unfulfilled private life with her man, which I found too simplistic and annoying, especially because I was then becoming aware of women's freedom of choices and their independence.

Probably because I was somewhat offended by Ruiko's assumption, I did not get back to her book and I had forgotten about Diane by the time I encountered her own work in the United States.

It was a portrait of a woman in the circus who swallowed a sword, standing, spreading her arms. Diane took the shot from right in front of her, and composed it so that when people look at the photograph, they will find a huge cross in the middle. I was stunned, tense, could not breathe. My palms were sweating. My knees trembled. Who was the photographer? I needed to find out about her.

I grabbed her biography (Patricia Bosworth, 1984) from the library, turned the pages impatiently, found more of her work and her self-portrait. All of a sudden, Ruiko's memoir flashed back to me and I could also picturize Diane's pale face and widened but frightened eyes. I turned more pages: photographs of her with her husband, Allan; of her pausing with her daughter, Doon; of her working in her loft—almost like a factory. The biography was not merely a patchwork of the pieces of facts. It was an art of patchworking and of contextualizing a person's life. At the same time, it allowed me to jump in anywhere in Diane's life, whenever and wherever I wanted to talk to her, to hug her, to cry with her.

Diane Arbus was born in 1923, as a daughter of wealthy family who owned a large department store on Fifth Avenue in New York City. She grew up on Central Park West in a Gothic apartment full of "useless experiences" (Bosworth, 1984, p. 50) and "gloomy, oppressive memories" (p. 50). Although Diane is reported to have shown her extraordinary sensitivity instead of pursuing her artistic talent she married Allan soon after graduation from high school. After years of walking on a thin line between a devoted mother/wife and an artist, Diane began to pursue "the forbidden" with her camera.

At a glance, Diane's life seems to be a stereotypical picture of a "midlife crisis," in which she suddenly terminated the marriage to a successful fashion photographer and started a totally new life, exploring her own talent and identity. This was the first impression that I had. I simply thought that Diane was one of those women who initially sacrificed their talents without knowing that they were doing so, suffered from the "problem that has no name" (Betty Friedan, 1963, pp. 11–27), then reawakened and rebelled against the traditional social order in order to retrieve their authentic selves. Maybe she was. I don't know. And even if she was, what difference does it make in the value of her work? She was not merely a strange artist who chased after scandalous subjects. Her impulses to photograph "freaks" did not come from her rejection of felt "unreality" of the fashion world but from her desire to scrutinize the world without evading facts, without evading what it really looks like.

> Freaks was a thing I photographed a lot. It was one of the first things I photographed and it had a terrific kind of excitement for me. I just used to adore them. I still do adore some of them. I don't quite mean they're my best friends but they made me feel a mixture of shame and awe. . . . Most people go through life dreading they'll have a traumatic experience. Freaks were born with their trauma. They've already passed their test in life. They're aristocrats. (Diane Arbus, 1972, p. 3)

According to the biographer, Diane had never called herself a feminist although people around her thought of her as "revolutionary." Diane talked frankly about her sexuality and her bodily sensations and was willing to take risks in order to satisfy her curiosity. She never compromised. She wanted and actually tried to experience everything that would be possible in life. She equated life with the process of discovery and, as a photographer, she challenged the traditional notion of documentary photography by pursuing her personal project: people "without their masks" (Bosworth, 1984, p. 178). Her subjects—midgets, nudists, transvestites, and so on—have been labelled as the perverse, and they were alienated from society. By deconstructing the boundary between the normal and the abnormal, Diane was questioning the *mystery of existence*.

While her photography gained public recognition, she came to be afraid of being labeled as a "weirdo" photojournalist. She was not looking for "sensational" subjects, but it was because she was able to capture the moment when people uncover their masks that her work turned out to be breathtaking. And yet Diane did not force or beg her subjects to unmask, but she tried to communicate with them on their terms. There was a mutual trust and fascination between the subjects and Diane. Diane did not "shoot" them or "take" their photograph. Together, they "made" a photograph. Hilton Kramer explains this possibility on the cover of *An Aperture Monograph* (Arbus, 1972):

> In her pictures nothing is improvised or merely "caught." The subjects face the camera with interest and patience. They are fully aware of the picture-making process. They collaborate. It is this element of participation, this suggestion of dialogue between the subject and the photographer, that gives these pictures their great dignity. And it is their dignity that is, I think, the source of the power. (cover)

Indeed, for Diane, they were not only the subjects of the photograph but more importantly, the subjects of the entire process of documenting a part of reality.

> I don't like to arrange things. If I stand in front of something, instead of arranging it, I arrange myself. (Arbus, 1972, p. 12)

> For me the subject of the picture is always more important than the picture. And more complicated. . . . I really think what it is, is what it's about. I mean it has to be of something. And what it's of is always more remarkable than what it is . . . I really believe there are things which nobody would see unless I photographed them. (Arbus, 1972, p. 15)

Shortly after I reencountered Diane in the U.S., I began to confront my subject—my own previous experience of anorexia. Feminist reexamination of the traditional discipline has been clamoring for recovering subjective experiences as a primary source of knowledge. (see Liz Stanley & Sue Wise, 1983; Dale Spender, 1981). The very fact that the objects of the research have always been called "subjects" regardless of the fact that they were the ones who were "observed," "measured," "manipulated," or "controled" was elucidated (see Sue Wilkinson, 1988). In my case, the subject and the object were one, but without working within a framework or a methodology of a traditional discipline, I did not know how to deal with that object within myself which begged for embodiment of its subjectivity.

Diane talked about her childhood experience as having a strong sense of unreality, and about the world which seemed to belong to the world but not to her. For more than 10 years, my anorexic experience had been unreal to me, even though I realized that my body had always existed and went through anorexic and postanorexic phases. The anorexic body described and explained in medical reports did not belong to me. That was not my own experience. Diane phrases this sensual fact as follows: "What I'm trying to describe is that it's impossible to get out of your skin into somebody else's" (Arbus, 1972, p. 2).

It was not entirely because of her curiosity that she had chosen freaks as her subjects. Freaks are alienated from the world. They do not belong to the world and that was a feeling that Diane herself shared as a child. She knew that she couldn't speak for them. She was aware of the fundamental limitation of her subjective reconstruction of reality (see Donna Haraway, 1988). She knew it takes both sides of the camera to make a photograph, to document their existence. That was why she invited her subjects as subjects, not as objects, into her work which, then became "their" work.

Little by little, I disentangled the knots of my anorexic experience which was also enigmatic and unreal to myself. In order to understand my own experience and the subjectivity of the object of my own research, I needed to let the anorexic body speak for itself. Neither my postanorexic body nor a medical report could speak for it. We worked together. I mean they—anorexic, postanorexic, and feminist bodies—found each other and embraced each other, valuing each other's existence.

In Diane's photographs, the subjects are often looking at the people who are looking at the photograph. I think this is another level of the subjects' inclusion into Diane's work. In other words, twins, transvestites, dwarfs, and freaks are facing to us who look at the photographs. Actually, we are not looking at the photographs but at them—twins, transvestites, dwarfs, freaks. We share the moment and the space and we realize that we exist together. In this way, Diane had already invited us into her work and their work which now become "our" work.

When I began writing about my exploration of my previous experience of anorexia, I never gave much thought to the audience. I was writing for my own sake and, especially, for the sake of my anorexic body who used to scream but was soundless. However, in the process of examining my experience, I realized the very reason why the medically legitimized version of anorexia felt unreal to me. After all, the report was not "equivalent" to anorexic women's experiences. The medical report was a version, a translation of a story that was not the whole. Where there are thousands of anorectics and postanorectics, there must be thousands of stories of anorexic experiences. I wanted to listen to these invisible and inaudible versions. In order to do so, I wanted to invite them into my story, into my search of the anorexic body so that we can explore our experiences together. Then, nobody could alienate parts of us, our bodies, or our experiences as "disturbed," "disordered," or "deficient." No. Not any more.

I learned from Diane. That:

Together, we work.

Together, we fill space.

Together, we animate the space.

The world lies between us.

Diane Arbus may have been an extraordinary artist, as society admits now. However, I would hesitate to call her an extraordinary woman because there is no such woman. The distinctions between what constitutes the ordinary and the extraordinary have become blurred, need to be questioned. Diane had fallen in love, become a 1940s child bride, raised two daughters, was caught between being a career woman and a perfect mother/wife, grew apart from her husband and found her lifework. She stands in the same ground where I stand, where my mother stands, where my grandmother stands. I have seen her moving through rooms. At some doors, she hesitated, poking her nose in. The others, she flung open and strided in. Every time I come closer to a door, I think of Diane, "Dee-ann" (Bosworth,

1984, p. 9). I think of her passion, her courage, her doubt, her fear, and her honesty to herself.

Diane Arbus killed herself in New York in the summer of 1971. I was a third grader, otenba girl, living on the other side of the globe.

REFERENCES

Arbus, Diane. (1972). *An aperture monograph*. New York: Millerton.

Armitage, Susan. (1987). Common ground—introduction to "American women's narratives." *Women's Studies, International Forum, 14*(1), 1–4.

Bosworth, Patricia. (1984). *Diane Arbus: A biography*. New York: Knopf.

Daly, Mary. (1978). *Gyn/ecology*. Boston: Beacon Press.

Freidan, Betty. (1963). *The Feminine Mystique*. New York: Dell.

Haraway, Donna. (1988). Situated knowledges: The science question in feminism and the privilege of partial perspective. *Feminist Studies, 14*(3), 575–599.

Spender, Dale. (1980). *Man made language*. New York: Routeledge & Kegan Paul.

Spender, Dale (Ed.). (1981). *Men's studies modified: The impact of feminism on the academic disciplines*. Oxford: Pergamon Press.

Stanley, Liz, & Wise, Sue. (1983). *Breaking out: Feminist consciousness and feminist research*. London: Routledge & Kegan Paul.

Wilkinson, Sue. (1988). The role of reflexivity in feminist psychology. *Women's Studies International Forum, 11*(5), 493–502.

Yoshida, Ruiko. (1983). *Jibun o sagashite tabi ni ikitemasu* [I live on the road, in search of myself.]. Tokyo: Kodansha.

Conclusion

Teresa Iles

In her introduction to *Rebecca West* (1985), Fay Weldon writes: "Better, if the biographer has a glimmer of the thin single consistent thread that runs through a life, to give up fact and take to fiction. It is as honourable a course as any" (p. 20). Her argument is that in real life you can search all around for the "because" to explain what people do, and never find it; "the facts" are less pieces of a jigsaw that fit together if they can all be found, rather they are like points which can be joined together in different dimensions and directions to show a complexity of aspects to the subject.

The writers of *All Sides of the Subject* have taken their own approaches to the dilemmas of writing biography. Their purposes are avowedly feminist and, while their subjects differ, there are some concerns that they share. Emphasis is on interpretation and on the grounds of their interests in the women whose lives they write. Their confidence in the reliability of the biographies they write comes from an optimistic approach to the certainty that "facts" never can stand separately from "a point of view." Meryn Stuart makes reference to Virginia Woolf's insight that women's lives have been fictionalized by men for centuries, and this has happily passed as factual authority on the female subject. The vast bulk of published work on women's lives (whether categorized as fiction or nonfiction) is of this nature. It is in this context that a feminist framework can be envisaged as unashamedly inventive of a multiplicity of new stories imaging/imagining women's lives.

Carolyn Heilbrun (1988, p. 20) also writes of the necessity for every movement to have sound intellectual underpinnings; certainly feminist writing, in belonging to the women's movement, is no different. The writers of *All Sides of the Subject* have made reference throughout to the ideas and theoretical positions which have been important to them. In some chapters these concerns are more explicitly intertwined with the process of writing biography. For example, Kathleen Barry and Liz Stanley both discuss the importance of staying with a practice that will never "fit" with the theoretical attitudes struck by "men's studies," just as the women whose lives they write contradicted the expectations for behavior in their time. They both show the consequences of privileging such theory as a body over the contextualized encounter and losing the interactive framework of biography. Carolyn Heilbrun's concern is not that the theoretical aspects of the project are not strong, but rather that "scholars will get lost in the intellectual ramifications of their disciplines," thus failing to address women who speak other languages, and creating another kind of exclusivity.

Following the same theme but in another way, the question of the concentration in biographical writing on "achieving" women is discussed by Rachel Gutiérrez and Elizabeth Crawford; both are aware how the concentration on documentary evidence such as letters, diaries, and records of public life inevitably reproduce the privilege of some women over others. Similarly, Miriam Kalman Harris' stuggle with valuation of the writing of her subject—whether she is "worthy enough" to be included within the bounds of published feminist literature and of biography—confronts the question as to where lines are to be drawn in this respect, and how the decision is to be made. Creating a class of "primary" women implies the creation of "the rest." Biographical work on the lives of "typical" women has more often been done by sociologists and historians; it has not been helpful to consider their work as "factual" in opposition to that of fiction writers. Happily, writing about women's lives transgresses many such divisions.

REFERENCES

Heilbrun, Carolyn. (1989). *Writing a woman's life.* London: Women's Press.
Weldon, Fay. (1985). *Rebecca West.* Harmondsworth: Penguin.

Index

Photograph by Judith Forman

About the Editor and Contributors

ABOUT THE EDITOR

Teresa Iles has organized her life in order that she can write and eat; she now teaches part time, with women's groups when possible. Her motivation has been a desire to understand more about ideas and their place in education; to this end she has done an M.A. and is working on an M.Phil, and attended a summer school on women and biography.

ABOUT THE CONTRIBUTORS

Kathleen Barry, PhD, is Associate Professor of Human Development at Penn State University and the author of *Susan B. Anthony, A Biography* (New York University Press, 1988; Ballantine paperback, 1990). She is also director of the Coalition Against the Traffic in Women, a nongovernmental organization resulting from her international study, *Female Sexual Slavery* (New York University Press, 1979), that is in consultative human rights status to the United Nations.

Anne-Kathrine Broch-Due is a Norwegian sociologist who works as a researcher at the University of Bergen. For a number of years she has been doing research on the labor market and education system from a feminist and life-course perspective.

Elizabeth Crawford: After a degree in History and Political Science from Exeter University, Elizabeth Crawford worked for 12 years in publishing before starting her own (small) business selling second-hand and antiquarian books by and about women. She is married and has three children.

Liz Dearden lives in Hebden Bridge, West Yorkshire. She is currently finishing an MA in Women's Studies at York University and shortly will start work with North West Arts Association in Manchester as Assistant to the Touring Officer. Her poetry has been published in *Iron, Writing Women, Cyphers, Singing Brink,* and *What Big Eyes You've Got.*

Margaret Forster was born in Carlisle in 1938. From the County High School she won an Open Scholarship to Sommerville College, Oxford where, in 1960, she was awarded an honors degree in History. In the same year she married Hunter Davies. Since 1963 Margaret Forster has worked as a novelist, biographer, and freelance literary critic, contributing regularly to Radio 4, notably "Woman's Hour" and "Start the Week;" TV Book Programs; newspapers—the TLS for instance—and magazines. She is the author of thirteen previous novels, including *Mother Can You Hear Me?* and *Private Papers* and has recently published a fourteenth, *Have the Men Had Enough,* based on her relationship with her dying mother-in-law. She has also published four works of nonfiction, most recently her acclaimed biography, *Elizabeth Barrett Browning,* and a selection of Elizabeth Barrett Browning's poetry. Margaret Forster lives in London with her husband. They have three children.

Rachel Gutiérrez is a Brazilian feminist writer and activist. She has a masters degree in philosophy and has published two books: *Feminism is Humanism* and *Women in Movement;* she also contributes monthly articles to a women's magazine. Rachel has been a concert performer and continues to give piano lessons. In 1986 she represented the feminist movement when she stood as a candidate for vice-governor of Rio de Janeiro. Her interest in feminist biography is based on her intention to write a book about Lou Andreas Salomé.

Miriam Kalman Harris is a writer/researcher. A reprint of *The Unpredictable Adventure* with her introduction will be published in 1992. She acknowledges Sallie Bingham and The Kentucky Foundation for Women for their support of her attendance to The Women's Studies Summer Institute at the University of London in July 1988. She is now editing an anthology of first person narratives and poetry, *Call It Courage: Women Transcending Violence.*

Pilar Hidalgo teaches English Literature at Malaga University, Spain. She is the author of four books on her subject and has published several articles on feminist criticism and the female tradition in the English novel. She is currently working on questions of female identity and self-representation in contemporary fiction.

Judith Jordan was raised on a midwestern farm by parents who took seriously Christian precepts and believed one should leave the world better than one found it. She was a child during the depression and remembers families walking along the highway. During the war she inspected fuses in a factory and worked in a navy shipyard as an electrician's helper. She was then graduated from college, got married, and continued to go to graduate schools, earning three master's degrees while bringing up three daughters. For many years she taught English in private schools in New York City. Now that she has more control over her time, she is writing short stories and is at work on a biography of Isabella Bird.

Takayo Mukai is a Japanese feminist who now lives in the United States. She has written an autobiographical thesis on her experience of anorexia nervosa. Her particular interest includes women's bodily experiences and how they are treated in a patriarchal society. She tries to approach the issue from a feminist as well as an Oriental woman's standpoint, in which she sees a lot of similarities. She also writes essays for the Women's Studies Association in Japan.

Ann Nilsen is a Norwegian sociologist doing feminist research on women teachers and engineers from a life-course perspective. She is a Research Fellow at the Department of Sociology, University of Bergen.

Abi Pirani is following a multimedia and interdisciplinary education in the arts and in Women's Studies; she now works as a freelance artist, writer and researcher, lecturer and parent. Her main interests focus on the daily lives we lead and how they affect and change our perspectives on the world.

Dale Spender is a feminist researcher/author who is concerned with making visible the individual and collective achievements of women. She has written extensively on women's intellectual and literary history (and its suppression), and because she wished to know more about women's biography she elected to set up a summer school course on the subject.

Liz Stanley is working class by birth, a northerner in England by choice, and a lesbian by luck, and she has taught in the Sociology Department at Manchester University, England, since 1977. She has written extensively on ideas about feminist research and feminist method, most recently in *Feminist Praxis: Research, Theory and Epistemology in Feminist Sociology* (Routledge, in press). Increasingly, her research interests focus on historical topics and on feminist auto/biography; she is currently researching some aspects of the presence of Mass observation, a project that encouraged members of the public to photograph and document everyday life, in Bolton in the 1930s. Whatever the apparent diversity of her research topics, her central and abiding sociological and feminist concern is with the processes by which "knowledge" is produced and contested.

Meryn Stuart is a Canadian feminist nurse/historian who teaches in the School of Nursing and in the Women's Studies program at the University of Ottawa, Ontario. She is writing a biography of an Ontario public health nurse in the 1920s and is attempting to make explicit some of the practical and theoretical issues involved. Her interest in this topic is fueled by a love/hate relationship with the practice of nursing and its contradictions.

THE ATHENE SERIES

An International Collection of Feminist Books
General Editors: Gloria Bowles, Renate Klein, and Janice Raymond
Consulting Editor: Dale Spender

MEN'S STUDIES MODIFIED: The Impact of Feminism on the Academic Disciplines
Dale Spender, editor

WOMAN'S NATURE: Rationalizations of Inequality
Marian Lowe and Ruth Hubbard, editors

MACHINA EX DEA: Feminist Perspectives on Technology
Joan Rothschild, editor

SCIENCE AND GENDER: A Critique of Biology and Its Theories on Women
Ruth Bleier

WOMAN IN THE MUSLIM UNCONSCIOUS
Fatna A. Sabbah

MEN'S IDEAS/WOMEN'S REALITIES: *Popular Science*, 1870—1915
Louise Michele Newman, editor

BLACK FEMINIST CRITICISM: Perspectives on Black Women Writers
Barbara Christian

THE SISTER BOND: A Feminist View of a Timeless Connection
Toni A.H. McNaron, editor

EDUCATING FOR PEACE: A Feminist Perspective
Birgit Brock-Utne

STOPPING RAPE: Successful Survival Strategies
Pauline B. Bart and Patricia H. O'Brien

TEACHING SCIENCE AND HEALTH FROM A FEMINIST PERSPECTIVE: A Practical Guide
Sue V. Rosser

FEMINIST APPROACHES TO SCIENCE
Ruth Bleier, editor

INSPIRING WOMEN: Reimagining the Muse
Mary K. DeShazer

MADE TO ORDER: The Myth of Reproductive and Genetic Progress
Patricia Spallone and Deborah Lynn Steinberg, editors

TEACHING TECHNOLOGY FROM A FEMINIST PERSPECTIVE: A Practical Guide
Joan Rothschild

FEMINISM WITHIN THE SCIENCE AND HEALTH CARE PROFESSIONS: Overcoming Resistance
Sue V. Rosser, editor

RUSSIAN WOMEN'S STUDIES: Essays on Sexism in Soviet Culture
Tatyana Mamonova

TAKING OUR TIME: Feminist Perspectives on Temporality
Frieda Johles Forman, editor, with Caoran Sowton

RADICAL VOICES: A Decade of Feminist Resistance from *Women's Studies International Forum*
Renate D. Klein and Deborah Lynn Steinberg, editors

THE WRITING OR THE SEX? or why you don't have to read women's writing to know it's no good
Dale Spender

THE RECURRING SILENT SPRING
H. Patricia Hynes

EXPOSING NUCLEAR PHALLACIES
Diana E.H. Russell, editor

FEMINIST PERSPECTIVES ON PEACE AND PEACE EDUCATION
Birgit Brock-Utne

THE SEXUAL LIBERALS AND THE ATTACK ON FEMINISM
Dorchen Leidholdt and Janice G. Raymond, editors

WHENCE THE GODDESSES: A Source Book
Miriam Robbins Dexter

NARODNIKI WOMEN: Russian Women Who Sacrificed Themselves for the Dream of Freedom
Margaret Maxwell

FEMALE-FRIENDLY SCIENCE: Applying Women's Studies Methods and Theories to Attract Students
Sue V. Rosser

SPEAKING FREELY: Unlearning the Lies of the Fathers' Tongues
Julia Penelope

BETWEEN WORLDS: Women Writers of Chinese Ancestry
Amy Ling

THE REFLOWERING OF THE GODDESS
Gloria Feman Orenstein

ALL SIDES OF THE SUBJECT: Women and Biography
Teresa Iles, editor